Central Banking in a Free Society

Central Banking in a Free Society

TIM CONGDON

The Institute of Economic Affairs

First published in Great Britain in 2009 by
The Institute of Economic Affairs
2 Lord North Street
Westminster
London SW1P 3LB
in association with Profile Books Ltd

The mission of the Institute of Economic Affairs is to improve public
understanding of the fundamental institutions of a free society, by analysing
and expounding the role of markets in solving economic and social problems.

A CIP catalogue record for this book is available from the British Library.

ISBN 978 0 255 36623 6

Many IEA publications are translated into languages other than English or
are reprinted. Permission to translate or to reprint should be sought from the
Director General at the address above.

Typeset in Stone by MacGuru Ltd
info@macguru.org.uk

Printed and bound in Great Britain by Hobbs the Printers

CONTENTS

THE AUTHOR

Tim Congdon is an economist and businessman who has for over thirty years been a strong advocate of sound money and free markets in the UK's public policy debates. Between 1992 and 1997 he was a member of the Treasury Panel of Independent Forecasters (the so-called 'wise men'), which advised the Chancellor of the Exchequer on economic policy. He founded Lombard Street Research, one of the City of London's leading economic research consultancies, in 1989, and was its managing director from 1989 to 2001 and its chief economist from 2001 to 2005. He has been a visiting professor at the Cardiff Business School and the City University Business School (now the Sir John Cass Business School). He was awarded the CBE for services to economic debate in 1997. His latest book, a collection of papers on *Keynes, the Keynesians and Monetarism*, was published in September 2007.

FOREWORD

The decision to give the Bank of England operational independence to control monetary policy in 1997 was widely regarded as an important step forward in ensuring that the UK had a credible monetary policy regime capable of keeping inflation under control. Gordon Brown's reforms of the Bank of England, however, involved two other aspects that have been given much less coverage. The first was to remove from the Bank responsibility for the supervision of the banking system and to hand it to the soon-to-be-formed Financial Services Authority. The second was to create a new agency of the Treasury to manage the national debt. In this monograph Tim Congdon argues that these two 'minor' reforms of the Bank of England had catastrophic effects in the financial market crisis of 2007 and 2008.

The author begins the monograph by discussing the Bank of England's role and purpose within a historical context. He rejects the arguments of the free-banking school, and argues that a central bank evolves naturally in a financial system where private agents are motivated by profit maximisation. If clearing banks are to economise on cash reserves, and make loans efficiently and cheaply, then, the author suggests, they need an institution that performs the functions of a modern-day central bank. Central banking allows banks to reduce their ratios of cash and capital to assets and the result is a reduction in loan margins and an increase in the flexibility of loan facilities, which benefits banks' customers.

These basic propositions will be controversial among some supporters of the free market who have accepted the arguments of Hayek, among others, for the denationalisation of money. The author's contribution to our understanding of the role of central banking in a market economy is, however, important. He is able to demonstrate how a coherent set of regulatory and monetary institutions can operate in a free society, even if the case for the denationalisation of the currency is not accepted.

The author accepts the argument that banking systems need regulation because the failure of one bank will have systemic effects on the payments system. Indeed, the failure of one bank can potentially bring the whole financial system down. The question then arises, 'Who should regulate the banking system?' Before extending a lender-of-last-resort loan the central bank must be able to distinguish between a bank that has liquidity problems and one that is genuinely insolvent. It must therefore have detailed information about the assets and liabilities of banks to which it may have to provide a last-resort loan. This establishes a prima facie case for banking regulation in the UK to be returned to the Bank of England. Lender-of-last-resort facilities and supervision of the banking system are complementary activities.

But would this not simply replace one state institution that regulates banking with another? Not necessarily. It is interesting that, as well as not questioning most aspects of Gordon Brown's dismembering of the Bank of England, few commentators question the ownership of the Bank. In fact, it has been nationalised only since 1946. From 1694 to 1946, the Bank of England was in private hands and did an extremely good job of maintaining financial stability. Why is it that no political party ever discusses the privatisation of the Bank of England, despite the fact that it was only nationalised by a radical government that was determined to take the 'commanding heights' of British industry under government control?

Privatising the Bank of England and ensuring that its capital is provided by commercial banks neatly square the circle. The lender-of-last-resort facility is a form of collective good, which all banks need to function efficiently, and which can be provided by an institution that is owned by and accountable to the banks that use the facility. The systemic effects of a bank failure on the rest of the banking system mean that regulation is another collective good which can be provided by the central bank for the mutual benefit of all banks in the system. If the Bank of England regulates banks too lightly, then there will be costs imposed on the central bank, which is owned by all other banks, as a result of the behaviour of bad banks. If the Bank of England regulates too heavily, then the banking system will be inefficient and banks will also suffer. A privately owned central bank is therefore subject to checks and balances. Regulation, under these proposals, would be provided by a market institution, not by a government body, and the degree and form of regulation will emerge from market processes. If a bank does not like the regulation imposed on it by the central bank, then that is no problem. It could simply operate outside the system and forgo liquidity support from the Bank of England. Indeed, it could seek such support elsewhere if it chose to do so and if another central bank wished to provide it. All its counterparties, however, would know the risks of dealing with a bank that chose not to be regulated by the Bank of England.

These proposals – returning banking regulation to the Bank

of England, privatising the Bank, and ensuring that it uses its lender-of-last-resort powers efficiently and generously – are self-consistent. They will not satisfy the free-banking school. They would, however, be a decisive step in a more liberal direction compared with our current position. The author argues that experience in the UK, over several decades, suggested that the proposed institutional structure can be effective in delivering the stability of the banking system. On the other hand, within little more than a decade Gordon Brown's reforms to the Bank of England led to the biggest bank run for well over a century.

The IEA commends this publication as an important contribution to our understanding of the role of a central bank in a free society.

The views expressed in this monograph are, as in all IEA publications, those of the authors and not those of the Institute (which has no corporate view), its managing trustees, Academic Advisory Council Members or senior staff.

PHILIP BOOTH
Editorial and Programme Director,
Institute of Economic Affairs
Professor of Insurance and Risk Management,
Sir John Cass Business School, City University
January 2009

SUMMARY

- Central banks are an essential component of a free and efficient banking system. They evolve naturally in a market economy and enable banks to economise on cash.
- Over time banks have reduced both liquidity and capital to what, at the time of the difficulties at Northern Rock, were historically low levels. This has allowed businesses and households to enjoy considerably reduced costs of borrowing from banks.
- The lender-of-last-resort role is a crucial function of central banks. The facility should be provided liberally to a bank in need of liquidity, just as was described by Bagehot in the nineteenth century.
- Very occasionally the central bank may wish to provide facilities to organisations outside the clearing bank system (such as AIG in the recent episode of financial instability), but this should always be done with a view to protecting the banking payments system.
- It is sometimes difficult to distinguish between banks that are insolvent and banks that are simply illiquid. Only the latter are entitled to lender-of-last-resort facilities as of right.
- Those responsible for making decisions about providing lender-of-last-resort facilities need to have experience of the banking system, and to have been involved with

the regulation and supervision of banks. Officialdom's performance in the Northern Rock affair suffered from lack of clarity about the respective roles of the Bank of England and the Financial Services Authority.

- This confusion about their roles was largely the result of Gordon Brown's dismemberment of the Bank of England in 1997. During the Northern Rock affair the Bank of England did not act promptly and efficiently as a banker to the banking system, as it had done in previous financial crises.

- Banks have to pay a penalty rate for, and to provide good-quality collateral against, lender-of-last-resort facilities. The claim by the present Governor of the Bank of England, Mervyn King, that last-resort assistance leads to moral hazard is overstated. By contrast, deposit insurance systems do create moral hazard. Such systems should be limited in scope and do not need to be pre-funded.

- The Bank of England needs to be active in providing lender-of-last-resort funds when necessary and should make this clear in contracts with clearing banks; it should be privatised and have its capital provided by clearing banks; and it should have returned to it the powers to regulate the banking system.

- This proposal would provide a stable set of incentives to keep regulation to the minimum necessary to maintain the stability of the banking system. Banks themselves, because they provide capital to the Bank of England, would suffer if one of their number were reckless and regulation too light. They would also suffer if there were over-regulation. The central bank, because it would be owned by the clearing banks, would have the right incentive structure to provide the appropriate degree of regulation.

TABLES AND FIGURES

AUTHOR'S PREFACE

This monograph is a response to very recent events, in particular the UK banking crisis that began in August 2007. However, some of the ideas – such as the argument that the evolution of central banks should be seen as the result of private agents' choices as they try to maximise profits – have been with me since the early 1980s. I am most grateful to the Institute of Economic Affairs for publishing the monograph since this argument is undoubtedly controversial in free-market circles. But one of my conclusions will, I expect, be welcome to economic liberals everywhere. This is that the central bank should be privatised and owned by the banking system, not by the state. I believe that central banks in private ownership would be subject to a better pattern of incentives, with checks and balances that would be more likely to keep them on the right course, than if they remain in the state's hands. More especially, my view is that the Bank of England's failure to act as a pre-emptive and efficient lender of last resort in the recent crisis can be blamed on the gradual erosion of its financial resources (i.e. its capital base), and of its powers and responsibilities, that occurred in the preceding six decades of public ownership. In my opinion the Bank's failure in this respect has had catastrophic consequences. It has both contributed to the severity of the latest cyclical downturn in demand, and caused long-term damage to the efficiency of our financial system and the international competitiveness of the City of London.

My main debt of gratitude is a negative one. I was dismayed in late 2007 and throughout 2008, first, by the volume of media commentary that was hostile to the British banking industry, and, second, to the assortment of wholly misguided policy prescriptions arising from this commentary. I suggest that the shambles of the British economy in early 2009 is – at least partly – the result of the translation of the commentariat's ideas into actual policy. (In qualification, I accept that blunders in financial policy have been made not just in the UK, but across the world.) So may I say 'thank you' to the various economic and financial journalists who made me so angry and spurred me into writing this work?

I am, as ever, grateful to Professor Charles Goodhart for his comments on an earlier version, and also to Professor Kevin Dowd and an anonymous referee for helpful criticisms. But I must emphasise that the views expressed here are very much my own.

I should declare a financial interest. I have owned shares in UK banks throughout the crisis and continue to do so, and am considerably poorer as a result. This preface was written in January 2009, but the text was finished in November 2008.

Central Banking in a Free Society

1 NEW DEBATES ON CENTRAL BANKING

In a modern economy the central bank – the bank that has been given the monopoly right to issue legal-tender notes (or 'cash') by the state – is generally understood to have two main objectives. The first, known as 'monetary stability', is to keep the value of the notes it issues steady in terms of goods and services, so that an index of prices does not change much over time; the second is to make arrangements with commercial banks which ensure that these organisations' deposit liabilities are always convertible at par into the legal-tender notes. This second objective is termed 'financial stability', although the phrase is sometimes used more broadly to encompass the avoidance of major disturbance in financial markets.[1]

Advocacy of monetary stability goes back to the late nineteenth century. The idea of an index number originated in the eighteenth century, but those involved in public affairs took

---

[1] In a celebrated article Anna Schwartz distinguished between 'real' and 'pseudo' financial crises, defining a real financial crisis as one in which the convertibility of deposits into currency (i.e. legal-tender notes) is widely regarded as being at risk. Writing in 1986, she said that 'All the phenomena of recent years that have been characterised as financial crises … are pseudo-financial crises.' See 'Real and pseudo-financial crises', in Anna J. Schwartz, *Money in Historical Perspective*, University of Chicago Press, Chicago and London, 1987, pp. 271–88, reprinted in Forrest Capie and Geoffrey Wood (eds), *Financial Crises and the World Banking System*, Macmillan, New York, 1986. The quotation is from pp. 271–2 of the 1987 book.

over a century to see its implications for economic policy. They did not quickly realise that the historically favoured approach – maintaining the convertibility of paper into a precious metal, usually gold, at a fixed price (i.e. the 'gold standard') – was not the alpha and omega of monetary management. Only in the opening decades of the twentieth century did such figures as John Maynard Keynes in Britain and Irving Fisher in the USA obtain widespread support for the view that policy should be directed to the stabilisation of the prices of a representative sample of goods and services, as measured in an index number.[2] It took a further 75 years or so before a strong commitment to focusing macroeconomic policy on the stability of a price index was made by the British government. In late 1992 Norman Lamont, the Chancellor of the Exchequer, announced a regime of 'inflation targets', with inflation (according to the retail price index minus mortgage rate effects) to be kept at an annual rate of 2.5 per cent.

At any rate, between 1992 and 2007 consumer price inflation was kept with hardly any interruption at between 2 and 2.5 per cent year after year, a remarkable improvement compared with the instability of price level changes in the preceding 90 years. Moreover, the performance of output and employment was benign throughout these years, confirming Friedman's view that no permanent trade-off prevailed between inflation and unemployment. It seemed that monetary stability not only was possible in theory, but had been achieved in practice. Between 1992 and

---

2   Irving Fisher first put forward his proposal to stabilise the general price level in his 1911 book *The Purchasing Power of Money* (Macmillan, New York). The theme was further developed in his 1920 *Stabilizing the Dollar* (Macmillan, New York, 1920) and was taken up by Keynes in articles in the *Guardian* which were brought together in his 1923 volume *A Tract on Monetary Reform* (Macmillan, London, 1923).

1997 the Conservative government of the day worked, with the assistance and advice of both the Treasury and the Bank of England, in pursuit of the inflation target.[3] In May 1997 the Bank of England was given operational independence to meet the inflation target, with its newly formed Monetary Policy Committee taking decisions on interest rates. In the early summer of 2007 it basked in the glory of delivering on-target inflation in its first decade of independence. Since monetary stability was a fact (for the time being, at least), the Bank seemed to have done exactly what it was supposed to do. In Goodhart's words, 'the structure of the MPC, and of the subsequent Bank of England Act, was excellently designed', while 'the MPC has been extremely successful in practice'.[4]

But – just as the ink was drying on all the congratulations about monetary stability – something went badly wrong on the financial stability front. Early 2007 had been a period of strain in international money markets, because of fears that a drop in US house prices would cut the value of certain mortgage-backed and -related securities. These instruments had a wide diversity of structures and indeed of names, including 'asset-backed securities' (ABS), 'collateralised debt obligations' (CDOs) and 'collateralised mortgage obligations' (CMOs). As noted in more detail in Chapter 6, the higher-quality securities were often accorded a

---

3 Treasury ministers received advice from the Treasury Panel of Independent Forecasters (the so-called 'wise men'), which might be seen as a forerunner of the Monetary Policy Committee. The author was a member of the Treasury Panel from its formation in December 1992 until it was wound up in May 1997.

4 Memorandum submitted by Professor (Emeritus) C. A. E. Goodhart, in Treasury Committee of the House of Commons, *The Monetary Policy Committee of the Bank of England: Ten years on*, The Stationery Office, London, vol. II: *Written evidence*, pp. 15–19. The quotation is from p. 15.

triple-A rating by the credit rating agencies and were regarded as being easily exchangeable for the cash issued by central banks.[5] In the jargon of the markets triple-A paper of this sort was deemed – or at any rate was initially deemed – to be highly 'liquid'.[6] On 9 August 2007 three money market mutual funds run by the French bank BNP Paribas, which had been large holders of ABS, CDOs and CMOs, declared that they had heavy losses and had to suspend redemptions. By implication, the instruments – even when accorded a triple-A rating – were not as good as cash, and might be risky and illiquid. This was an unexpected shock to bank managements around the world. In the words of one money manager, echoing Donald Rumsfeld on the invasion of Iraq, '… we are discovering there are a lot more unknown unknowns than anyone thought'.[7]

In the UK all banks had been big issuers of ABS, CDOs and related securities in 2005 and 2006, but one particular category of bank – mortgage banks, including a trio of former building

---

5   A little more detail may be helpful. Typically, ABS and CDOs were sold as products of so-called 'structured finance'. Claims on pools of mortgage-backed (or other asset-backed) securities were split up, with one tranche having a first claim on the pool and hence little risk of default, a second tranche the next claim, and so on. Most commercial banks held only the high-quality tranches, unless they had been involved in underwriting the securities, in which case they might hold lower-quality tranches because they had been unable to find buyers.

6   The term 'liquid' is one of the most overused and ambiguous in monetary economics. The classic definition was given by Keynes in *The Treatise on Money*, where he said that among banks' assets bills are more liquid than 'investments' (i.e. government bonds) because they are 'more certainly realisable at short notice without loss' (John Maynard Keynes, *Treatise on Money*, Macmillan, London, 1930, vol. 2: *The Applied Theory of Money*, p. 67). See John Hicks, *A Market Theory of Money*, Oxford University Press, Oxford, 1989, p. 61, for an appreciation of Keynes's definition. Hicks believed that Keynes's reference in 1930 may have been the first by any economist to the notion of 'liquidity'.

7   Alex Brummer, *The Crunch*, Random House Business Books, London, 2008, p. 61.

societies, Northern Rock, Alliance & Leicester, and Bradford & Bingley – had been particularly active. The announcement from the French money market funds on 9 August caused a virtual cessation of new ABS and CDO issues, and so cut off a major source of funds for these institutions. Northern Rock's management quickly realised that a securities issue it had planned for September could no longer proceed and that over the next few months it would face serious difficulties in financing its assets. It informed its regulator, the Financial Services Authority, of its looming problem on 13 August. The subsequent shenanigans are discussed in more detail in Chapter 6.

Traditionally bank regulation had been a responsibility of the Bank of England, but that had been changed by legislation in 1998 which split the job between the so-called 'Tripartite Authorities' (the FSA, the Bank and the Treasury). On 13 September an announcement was due that the Bank of England would provide loan support for Northern Rock. The announcement was somehow leaked in advance to Robert Peston of the BBC, who proceeded to put out a 'scoop', which left viewers and listeners with the mistaken impression that Northern Rock was bust. Northern Rock's retail depositors started to pull out cash on a large scale. The momentum of the withdrawals was reinforced by the breakdown of Northern Rock's website (because it was receiving too many hits) and television pictures of queues forming outside Northern Rock branches.[8]

In these circumstances the only method of maintaining the full

---

[8]   Apart from Brummer's excellent narrative account of these events, there are the Treasury Committee's report, *The Run on the Rock*, referenced in the next footnote, and an insider version, Brian Walters, *The Fall of Northern Rock*, Harriman House, Petersfield, 2008.

convertibility of deposits into cash was for Northern Rock to draw on its loan facility at the Bank of England. Later Northern Rock was described, notably by the Bank's governor, Mervyn King, as 'reckless' in its reliance on the *wholesale* funding of its mortgage assets.[9] In fact, a major counterpart to the Bank's loan to Northern Rock, which eventually reached about £30 billion, was a collapse in its *retail* deposits (see Table 1). Most serious analysts, backed up by comments from the UK's senior bank regulators, agreed that Northern Rock's mortgage assets were of good quality, and that eventually the bank ought to be able to repay its deposits and wholesale liabilities. By implication, the blame for the first big run on a British bank's deposits lay heavily with incompetent handling of the crisis by the Tripartite Authorities in August and September 2007. Whereas the Bank of England's achievement of monetary stability was impressive, there had been a clear failure in the delivery of financial stability.

Table 1 **The hole in Northern Rock's balance sheet**

At 31 December 2007 Northern Rock owed £28.5 billion to the Bank of England, whereas a year earlier it had owed the Bank nothing. In terms of counterparts, the loan had been necessitated by three developments.

	£ billion
Increase in Northern Rock's assets	8.8
Decrease in retail 'customer accounts'	15.3
Decrease in other liabilities, mostly wholesale	4.4
Total of three developments	28.5

Source: Northern Rock reports and accounts

9   See the evidence given by King and Professor Willem Buiter, as summarised on p. 18 of vol. 1 of the Treasury Committee's *The Run on the Rock: 5th report of session 2007/8*, The Stationery Office, London, 2008.

Since modern Britain was unfamiliar with bank runs, politicians, commentators, journalists and even bankers themselves were unsure about the appropriate policy response. One feature of the situation that was new, conspicuous and unexpected was the Bank of England's large loan to Northern Rock.[10] Since the Bank of England had been owned by the state since its nationalisation in 1946, the loan was widely characterised as 'government money'. A recurrent theme in media coverage was that 'Northern Rock is receiving government money', as if the Bank's loan to Northern Rock were analogous to public expenditure on education and health. According to John Kay in his column in the *Financial Times*, writing in July 2008, 'Still the bills roll in. Taxpayers have already written impressively large cheques for Northern Rock ...'[11] This notion was often associated with the allegation that the government was prepared to dole out money to help 'The City', but that it was mean towards nurses and teachers, whose pay increases were being restricted as part of the larger effort to curb public expenditure.

---

10 In nominal terms the Bank of England's loan to Northern Rock was unprecedented in terms of size. Its exposure relative to risk in the private sector, however, was not unprecedented relative to GDP. As noted by Bagehot in *Lombard Street*, the Bank of England's loans on 'private securities' jumped in the 1866 crisis from £18.5 million to £33.4 million. Total advances on 'proper security' in the same crisis were claimed by the Bank itself to amount to £45 million. With GDP in 1866 estimated at £966 million, the 1866 credit extensions were therefore between 1.5 and 4.5 per cent of GDP, equivalent in today's terms to just over £20 billion and just under £65 billion. Walter Bagehot, *Lombard Street*, vol. IX in Norman St John-Stevas (ed.), *The Collected Works of Walter Bagehot*, The Economist, London, 1978, originally published in 1873, pp. 78, 132, and B. R. Mitchell, *British Historical Statistics*, Cambridge University Press, Cambridge, 1988, p. 836. The secondary banking crisis in the mid-1970s also exposed the Bank of England to large possible losses.

11 John Kay, 'Fannie Mae and the limits of public obligation', *Financial Times*, 16 July 2008.

The media hubbub was mostly silly, but the Northern Rock affair did raise wider issues. In particular, a basic question for future public policy was 'how should the state organise the regulation of banks and the financial system to prevent a repeat of the Northern Rock fiasco?' To some observers the cause of the run in September 2007 was the low level of deposit insurance in the UK. On this view retail depositors pulled their money out of Northern Rock because they were certain of receiving back 100p in the £ only on the first £2,000 of deposits. On the next £33,000 they would receive back only 90p in the £ and on sums above £35,000 they were, in the extreme, liable to lose the entire amount deposited. Given the alarmist tone of the Peston leak on 13 September, the rush to withdraw money over the next few days was rational, even if misinformed and unnecessary.[12] The answer seemed to lie in improved terms for deposit insurance. This was certainly one message in evidence given by King to the Treasury Committee of the House of Commons on 20 September. The Committee's report, *The Run on the Rock*, which appeared in January 2008, duly emphasised the position of depositor protection in the British financial system and recommended 'the establishment of a Deposit Protection Fund to be funded by participating institutions'.[13]

---

12 The usual reference here is to a classic article by Diamond and Dybvig, which shows why an individual depositor is rational to withdraw funds from a bank he believes to be solvent, if he also believes that other depositors will withdraw funds on a large scale before him (Douglas W. Diamond and Philip H. Dybvig, 'Bank runs, deposit insurance and liquidity', *Journal of Political Economy*, University of Chicago Press, Chicago, 91(3), 1983). The Diamond and Dybvig article provided a scholarly case for deposit insurance and argued that lender-of-last-resort assistance to banks created problems of moral hazard in their asset selection. The same themes appear in Mervyn King's speeches.

13 Treasury Committee, op. cit., vol. 1, p. 118.

Concern was expressed that, even if depositors eventually received 100p in the £, they might get their money back only after a delay. In order that such delays could be avoided, the argument was heard that the Deposit Protection Fund should be financed in advance. This raised several new questions, however, notably how the 'participating institutions' were to raise the funds that were to be injected into the Deposit Protection Fund. In June 2008 King spoke at the British Bankers' Association annual conference and proposed to the 350 delegates that 'Some element of pre-funding is natural'.[14] Since the banks were at the same time trying to raise capital on the stock market by rights issues, the suggested requirement to pre-fund a new scheme (which would absorb some of the rights issue money) was unwelcome to them, to say the least. One result was a further deterioration of relations between King and leading bankers.

By the summer of 2008 relations between the Bank of England and Britain's banks had never been worse. The tensions were aggravated by the strong resentment felt – in both the Treasury and the Bank of England – at the wide disparity between their own public sector salaries and the often fantastic incomes earned by leading figures in the banking industry. Influential journalists, such as Martin Wolf, the chief economic commentator on the *Financial Times*, urged that financial regulators ought to introduce controls on bankers' pay. In April 2008 the Institute of International Finance, said to represent 375 of 'the world's largest financial companies', responded to public hostility by acknowledging that banks had taken too many risks and paid excessive

---

14 Christine Selb, 'King clashes with banks by urging advance funding of compensation', *The Times*, 11 June 2008, and Christine Selb et al., 'Banks may be forced to pump billions into savings compensation scheme', *The Times*, 30 June 2008.

bonuses.[15] Banks' requests for help from the Bank of England, and their resistance to extra imposts such as the advance money for the Deposit Protection Fund, were seen as special pleading. Along with the allegation that Northern Rock had taken up scarce 'government money', numerous media reports represented the banks as greedy and inefficient.

The crisis reached a new level of intensity in September and October 2008. By then the leading British banking groups had announced their results for the first half of 2008, and all of them were profitable and solvent. Nevertheless, the Tripartite Authorities got it into their heads that British banks were undercapitalised and at risk of 'going bust'. The banks were dragooned into a recapitalisation exercise, in which they were forced to sell preference shares to the government at an interest rate of 12 per cent. (In mitigation, it has to be said that similar programmes of bank recapitalisation were organised in other countries, but nowhere was the government as vindictive towards the banks as in the UK. In the USA, where several banks were indeed close to insolvency and actually insolvent, the government also bought bank preference shares in a similar recapitalisation programme, but it charged only 5 per cent.)[16]

The prime minister, Gordon Brown, somehow managed to persuade the media that bank recapitalisation, for which he

---

15 Krishna Guha and Chris Giles, 'Blame us for crisis, say leading bankers', *Financial Times*, 10 April 2008.

16 The issuance of preference shares to the state by banks in difficulty is not new. It was adopted in the USA by the Reconstruction Finance Corporation from 1933, to help in the recapitalisation of the US banking system. The point was noted in the author's article 'There is nothing magic about this Keynesian fad', *Spectator*, 25 October 2008. The issuance of preference shares by the finance ministry could be regarded as a kind of lender-of-last-resort loan, although it does not come from the central bank.

took personal credit, was a masterstroke. It certainly pandered to widespread anti-bank sentiment in the chattering elite. Media opinion has to some extent already translated into legislative and regulatory action, such as the 2008 Banking Reform Act, which will in the first instance damage bank profitability. The effects in the longer run will include a rise in the cost of banking services to companies and individuals, and the transfer of internationally mobile banking activities from the UK (particularly from London) to other countries. Given the contribution that financial services have made to economic growth in the UK over the last 40 years, this relocation of activities may prove a national disaster. Historically, the Bank of England had a friendly and cooperative relationship with Britain's banks, and this was one factor in the competitiveness of the City of London relative to other financial centres.

The purpose of this study is to argue for a redefinition of the Bank of England's position in the British financial system, in order to improve its delivery of financial stability. An underlying theme throughout will be that many of the Bank's traditional and established arrangements, jettisoned over the last decade, often for no clear reason, had a strong functional rationale. In his evidence to the Treasury Committee on 20 September, King offered his perspective on the Northern Rock run. The thrust of his remarks was that direct measures of deposit protection, including the expansion of deposit insurance already mentioned, should have more prominence in the pursuit of financial stability than in the past. By contrast, he had little to say about the Bank's work as lender of last resort. Implicitly, the lender-of-last-resort role was to be demoted. In its report about *The Run on the Rock* the Treasury Committee devoted just one page to the lender-of-last-resort function of central banks, compared with a full chapter of sixteen pages and much other material to deposit protection. Even this page damned by faint praise, opining that – because the publicity arising from the announcement on 14 September had damaged depositors' confidence in Northern Rock and so sparked the run – 'the level of stigmatisation now attached to [a lender-of-last-resort] facility is such that its effectiveness must be in doubt'.[17]

The argument of this study will be that, on the contrary, the Bank of England's responsibility to act as lender of last resort – its responsibility, in other words, to lend to solvent banks when they are short of cash – is one of its defining tasks. Arguably both deposit insurance and last-resort lending have a role, and a balance has to be struck over their relative weight in financial regulation. The emphasis here is on the advantages of the lender-of-last-resort role and the disadvantages of deposit insurance. The implications for the Bank of England's structure are drawn out in Chapter 7, which includes the radical recommendation that it ought to be privatised if it is to be most effective in the delivery of financial stability.

The correct specification of the central bank's lender-of-last-resort role has been controversial since the term was first used by Sir Francis Baring in 1797. The classic formula, given by Walter Bagehot in his 1873 *Lombard Street*, was that in a crisis the central bank should lend at a penalty rate without limit against good collateral. The Bagehot principle will be reviewed in Chapter 5 and King's attitude towards it is discussed in Chapter 6. But an account of the development of banking and central banking, and an explanation of how the wider economy benefits from increased

---

17   Treasury Committee, op. cit., vol. 1, p. 86.

financial intermediation, is needed first. These form the subject matter of the next three chapters.

The author of this study is probably best known as an advocate of monetary control to reduce inflation. Apart from a brief reference to the risks of debt deflation in Chapter 7, the subject of monetary stability is not explicitly considered. No elaborate reasoning is necessary, however, to defend the proposition that a nation with a stable financial system is far more likely to enjoy monetary stability than a nation where the banks are footballs in the political debate, and can be kicked around at the whim of politicians, civil servants and newspaper columnists.

This study is illustrated mostly by events that have happened in the UK. It is hoped that – with a little tweaking of names, dates and phrases – the analysis of central banking presented here is relevant to almost any country.

2 CENTRAL BANKING: SPONTANEOUS OR IMPOSED?

Central banks are relatively modern institutions, with the notion of 'a central bank' distinct from the rest of the banking system being unknown before the nineteenth century. Because of their modernity, more or less complete historical records to chronicle their progress are available and their origins ought to be uncontroversial. But that is not the case. Instead two conflicting schools of thought have for the last 25 years or so been battling over the correct way to characterise the development of central banking. This battle, of much intellectual interest in its own right, is also relevant to the design of central banks' structure and operations.

Do central banks develop spontaneously?

The first school of thought proposes what might be termed 'the imposed order' model of central banking development. Its argument is that a central bank is the creation of government, since only government can give an institution the right to issue legal-tender notes. The central bank is also often granted powers, by legislation or executive order, to regulate privately owned banks for reasons of wider public policy. Such regulations may include constraints on banks' asset composition, including – for example – requirements that banks hold high ratios of their total assets in the form of cash (i.e. legal-tender money plus a balance at the central bank) and/or government securities. The regulations may appear to be justified on prudential grounds, in that they improve banks' ability to repay deposits at par. But, according to the imposed-order model, their true purpose is to divert resources to the state. Indeed, in the more extreme statements of the imposed-order model, the central bank is little more than a tax-collecting agency.[1] More generally, according to this school of thought, central banks do not arise 'from below', from the felt and clearly articulated needs of individual citizens and private companies. Instead they are imposed 'from above'; they are derived from 'forces outside the system (or 'exogenously')'.[2]

The alternative school of thought begins by noting that banking emerged many centuries before the establishment of central banks and then emphasises that central banks provide services to commercial banks. From the very start of banking a key management objective was to reduce the ratio of cash (which does not earn interest) to as low a ratio of total assets as possible, while maintaining the convertibility of deposits into cash. In pursuit of this objective the more risk-prone banks tended to keep a proportion of their cash with particularly reliable and well-capitalised banks, so that the latter organisations became 'bankers' banks'. By extension the central bank is interpreted as the ultimate 'bankers' bank', the safest bank of all. In any society government is special,

---

[1]   For the link between budget deficits and the levying of an inflation tax, see Tim Congdon, 'The link between budget deficits and inflation: some contrasts between developed and developing countries', in Michael J. Boskin et al. (eds), *Private Saving and Public Debt*, Blackwell, Oxford and New York, 1987, pp. 72–91, and, in particular, p. 77.

[2]   The phrase is taken from Hayek. See Friedrich A. Hayek, *Law, Legislation and Liberty*, Routledge & Kegan Paul, London, 1973, vol. 1: *Rules and Order*, p. 36.

in that it monopolises the legitimate use of force. Almost inevitably, the banker to the government must therefore be that safest bank. It follows that – spontaneously, naturally – the bankers' bank and the banker to the government become one and the same institution, the central bank. Since banks benefit from the services provided by a central bank, a central bank arises 'from below', from the commercial motivations of private sector agents. Central banking is therefore to be seen as part of the 'spontaneous order'; it may be analysed as a 'self-organising or self-generating system' which evolves from 'endogenous' pressures as a variety of agents, many of whom do not know each other, interact to their mutual advantage.[3]

The debate between the 'imposed order' and 'spontaneous order' schools has enlivened academic journals and spawned a number of fascinating monographs. Advocates of the imposed-order point of view often go farther, by proposing that central banking should be replaced by what they term 'free banking'. According to Vera Smith, a seminal contributor to the imposed-order school, free banking 'denotes a regime where note-issuing banks are allowed to set up in the same way as any other type of business enterprise, so long as they comply with the general company law'.[4] More concisely, free banking would involve the repeal of the legal tender laws.[5] Since legal-tender notes could no longer exist, a central bank – defined in particular by its

---

3   The phrases are again taken from Hayek, ibid., vol. 1, p. 37.

4   Vera C. Smith, *The Rationale of Central Banking*, Liberty Press, Indianapolis, 1990 (originally published in London by P. S. King & Son, 1936), p. 169.

5   This has numerous implications, leading to a large literature. The International Library of Macroeconomic and Financial History, published by Edward Elgar, has three volumes on *Free Banking* under the editorship of Lawrence White, which contain no fewer than 55 articles.

possession of the monopoly right to issue such notes – also could not exist. In an astute piece of brand-building, Hayek said that free banking would amount to 'the denationalisation of money'.[6]

There is no room here to present all the facts – largely, the historical facts – that are at issue between the two schools. Nevertheless, some key points are straightforward and arguably go some way to settling the matters in contention. Not only does the central bank provide services to commercial banks, but also the terms and conditions relating to these services have been determined by voluntary negotiations over many decades between the central bank and privately owned banks.[7] It follows that the spontaneous-order school is substantially correct. In any case, a fair comment is that contemporary policymakers and business leaders have shown little interest in free banking. To that extent the debates between the imposed-order and spontaneous-order schools are remote from today's institutional realities, and lack plausibility.[8]

Moreover, the sharpness of the distinction between the imposed and spontaneous models is harder to sustain in practice than it is in theory. The history of the Bank of England, founded in 1694 and often said to be the oldest central bank, illustrates the

6   Hayek, *The Denationalisation of Money*, Hobart Paper 70, Institute of Economic Affairs, London, 1976.

7   Sometimes commercial banks are forced to accept rules and regulations, and their role in negotiations with the central bank is therefore involuntary. But that was not the historical norm in the UK in peacetime. This is part of the reason why certain recent events, such as the recapitalisation exercise in October 2008 which was imposed on the banks against their will, were so disturbing.

8   'The failure to recognize that we are in unexplored terrain gives an air of unreality and paradox to the discussion of private money and free banking.' Quotation from p. 311 of Milton Friedman and Anna Schwartz, 'Has government any role in money?', in Anna Schwartz, *Money in Historical Perspective*, University of Chicago Press, Chicago and London, 1987, pp. 289–314.

fuzziness of the concepts at play.[9] In her influential book on *The Rationale of Central Banking*, Smith noted that 'The early history of the Bank was a series of exchanges of favours between a needy Government and an accommodating corporation', including the running of the government's own balances and the privilege of limited liability. In her view limited liability was an advantage 'denied to all other banking associations for another one and a half centuries'.[10] This overlooked two points. First, the very concept of a central bank was not fully clarified in the 161 years between the Bank's founding and the first limited liability legislation, which on its passage in 1855 extended the right to limited liability to most new companies. Second, the Bank of England obtained its monopoly of note issuance only after 1826, no less than 132 years from its establishment. Further, it was in the decades following its monopolisation of the note issue that the Bank lost its leadership, in terms of size and profitability, in the British banking system.

Smith was right that, since the privileges given to the Bank of England in 1694 benefited several generations of shareholders, the government of the day and the Bank's shareholders could be construed as imposing their institution 'from above'. But she ought also to have acknowledged that it was only with the granting of the note-issue monopoly that the Bank of England became more definitely a modern central bank. Further, in the third quarter of the nineteenth century both the banking industry and those concerned with public policymaking in this

9   For notes on the histories of the leading central banks, see pp. 123–231 of Forrest Capie et al. (eds), *The Future of Central Banking*, Cambridge University Press, Cambridge, 1994. The Swedish Riksbank, today the central bank of Sweden, is sometimes said to be an older 'central bank' than the Bank of England. But neither of them was a central bank when they were established.

10   Smith, op. cit., p. 12.

field understood that the rapid expansion of the Bank's note issue could lead to overissue and inflation, and so endanger monetary stability. So the Bank ceased to be a profit-maximising institution and increasingly resembled a modern central bank. For the public good it *restricted* its lending to non-bank private agents and *reduced* returns to its own shareholders.[11] This acceptance of a public policy role was at least partly because of pressures from bankers and merchants in the City of London, pressures which were surely 'from below'.

Importance of banks' profit-maximisation objective

Whatever the rights and wrongs of the debate, one theme does emerge clearly from the last section. This is that the evolution of the banking industry's structure is influenced by the objective of profit maximisation in privately owned financial institutions. Discussions about the choice of monetary and banking regimes often pivot on wider political commitments to individual liberty, social justice and so on. These have their place and will be recalled in the final chapter. But it must not be forgotten that different structures of the banking industry affect banks' profits. Of course, bankers are likely to favour arrangements that boost their profits and oppose those which cut them. The analysis in the rest of this chapter and in Chapter 3 will turn on a simple formula for the determination of banks' 'loan margins', and it will assume

11 Bagehot's insistence in the 1870s that the Bank of England could not act as a simple profit-maximiser led to a famous dispute with Thomas Hankey, a director of the Bank of England. For Hankey's point of view, see a reprint of his essay 'Banking in connection with the currency and the Bank of England', in Michael Collins (ed.), *Central Banking in History*, Edward Elgar, Aldershot, UK, and Brookfield, USA, 1993, vol. 1, pp. 194–235. See, particularly, pp. 222–5.

that banks' executives set loan margins in order to target certain rates of return on capital. Rather than relying on a vague appeal to 'freedom' or some other abstract ideal, the analysis will be set in a framework of profit maximisation. Nevertheless, a key desideratum will be the identification of the social costs and benefits of central banking.

Bank loans are risky and costly to organise, and they are financed by deposits on at least part of which interest is payable. It is clear that revenues (i.e. net interest margin, fees and other income) must be sufficient at least to cover the following list of items:

- an allowance for likely loan losses;
- the costs of organising the loans and maintaining the money transmission infrastructure which enables banks to collect deposits; and
- the marginal cost of funds to the lending bank, in terms of the interest rate paid on deposits or other finance.

Loan losses in most banking industries are typically under 1 per cent of assets in any one year, and for many banks over extended periods of years have been under 0.25 per cent.[12] For simplicity, the rate of loan loss is ignored in the rest of this chapter. In the real world the costs of organising loans are substantial, but they are largely met or exceeded by arrangement fees. For banks with extensive branch networks and a major role in the payments

---

[12] The write-off rate on the loan assets of the much-maligned Northern Rock in the first half of 2007 was 0.01 per cent, although a larger charge (of almost 0.12 per cent of mean advances to customers) was made. See section on 'Loan loss impairment' in Northern Rock's *Interim Results*, published on 25 July 2007.

mechanism, the costs of collecting and managing deposits are also substantial, but they are assumed here to be zero to ease the exposition. With the assumptions of nil loan losses and zero running costs, the average return on banks' assets would still not be identical to the loan margin if assets consisted of bonds and securities as well as loans. Nevertheless, the concepts must be closely related in a world – such as that of today – in which banks' assets are dominated by their loan portfolios. In the rest of this paper the phrases 'return on bank assets' and 'loan margin' are used interchangeably in order to facilitate the discussion, even though they are not the same in practice. (Obviously, loan margins need to be adjusted upwards to deliver a particular 'return on assets' if allowance has to be made for loan losses and bank running costs.)

The list of costs set out in the last paragraph applies to all types of credit institution. But many such institutions – including, for example, hire purchase companies and specialist leasing businesses – are not banks. Without entering too deeply into the vexed question 'what is a bank?', the distinctive characteristics of banks may be understood to include the ability to take and repay cash deposits over the counter, and an obligation to maintain a cushion of capital against possible loans losses which further protects depositors' interests. Historically cash reserves, both in the form of 'vault cash' and in a balance at the central bank, have not paid interest, but they are essential for retail deposit-taking.[13] It follows that, for any given loan margin (which may be measured as a percentage of loan assets), the rate of return on assets is a

13 The current fashion is for central banks to introduce the payment of interest on balances held with it, subject to various restrictions which are intended to facilitate their control over short-term interest rates. While this change is of great importance to banks' cash-holding behaviour, a proper discussion would take up too much space.

positive function of the ratio of non cash-earning assets to total assets. Plainly the rate of return on capital depends on both the rate of return on assets and the ratio of capital to assets.

The argument is easily stated in algebraic terms. Let a bank's assets be split between cash, C, with c representing the ratio of cash to assets, and earning assets or loans, L. Then total assets A = C + L or A = c.A +L. So L = (1 − c).A. Profits (P) are equal to the loan margin or profit 'spread' on assets, s, multiplied by the earning assets, L, or

$$P = s.L = s.(1 - c).A,$$

while the rate of return on capital (K) is P/K, which is

$$P/K = s.(1 - c).A/K.$$

So

$$s = P/K. (1/[1 - c]). K/A.$$

It is clear that, if the loan margin is given, the rate of return on capital is inversely related to the cash/assets ratio (or indeed in practice the cash/deposits ratio) and the capital/assets ratio. As Phillips remarked in his 1921 classic on *Bank Credit*, 'the essence' of banking 'consists in the practice of extending loans far in excess of either the capital or the cash holding of the bank in question'.[14] By implication, bankers are likely to support any developments, in technology or institutions, including the institutional

---

14   A. W. Phillips, *Bank Credit*, Macmillan, New York, 1921, p. 13.

relationships within their own industry, which enable them to lower their cash/deposits ratio (i.e. their 'liquidity') and their capital/assets ratio (i.e. their 'solvency'). The next chapter discusses the long-run trends in banks' liquidity and solvency, with particular emphasis on the UK, although with some discussion of the role of clearing-house associations in the USA before the establishment of the Federal Reserve.

3 THE EVOLUTION OF BANKING SYSTEMS

Banking evolved from the safe keeping of money.[1] In stylised accounts of the subject people left deposits of a widely recognised monetary commodity (usually a precious metal or 'bullion', such as gold and silver) with a specialist in safe keeping, such as a goldsmith. Initially the deposit was backed 100 per cent by the assumedly safe 'hard' monetary asset. Over time the notes that acknowledged the deposits were used in transactions instead of bullion, while bankers found that they could make loans in their note liabilities instead of tangible gold or silver. By issuing note liabilities without metal backing, the ratio of bullion to total liabilities fell from 100 per cent or more to markedly lower levels. Nowadays the safe monetary asset – the so-called 'monetary base' – is no longer a precious metal, but the legal-tender notes issued by the central bank. But, like gold or silver, legal-tender notes do not pay interest. Because notes are not earning assets, modern banks want to reduce the ratio of cash to their earning assets, in the same way as goldsmiths in embryonic banking.

---

1   According to the so-called 'de Roover thesis', as a matter of historical fact banking began as a by-product of foreign exchange dealing, with the foreign exchange dealer acting occasionally as a custodian. Interest on deposits was paid from an early stage. See Julius Kirshner (ed.), *Banking, Business and Economic Thought: Selected Studies of Raymond de Roover*, University of Chicago Press, Chicago and London, 1974, pp. 200–201.

Cash in early banking

Early banks often had cash/asset ratios of over 50 per cent. One example is provided by Scottish banking in the middle of the eighteenth century, which is a favourite topic of the advocates of 'free banking'. Indeed, Scottish banking in early modern times was characterised by so-called 'note wars', in which a bank jealous of a rival would encourage business associates to hand over notes and withdraw bullion from that rival so that its bullion would be exhausted![2] But over time banks came to realise that cooperation, as well as competition, had its merits. As well as offering to repay deposits over the counter, banks undertook to make cash payments to third parties on behalf of their customers. So individual A would not need to withdraw £100 of notes from bank X in order to pay them to individual B, who then deposited them at bank Y. Instead bank X would debit £100 from A's account and pay £100 in notes to bank Y, in order that bank Y would credit £100 to B's account. Settling the transaction between A and B via the banks would save legwork and time, particularly if the two banks were located close to each other in a financial metropolis.

So early banking was associated with the establishment of 'note exchanges'. But the physical counting, bundling and transporting of notes remained resource intensive. Real-world payments have always consisted of complicated criss-cross patterns of debits and credits, with most agents having gross incomings and outgoings that are a multiple of the change in their net cash position. Suppose – in our example – that individual C, also with an account at bank Y, wants to make a payment of £100 to individual A. One procedure would be for C to withdraw

---

2   Charles W. Munn, 'The origins of the Scottish note exchange', *Three Banks Review*, 102, June 1974, pp. 45–60. See, particularly, pp. 50–52.

£100 in notes from bank Y and to pay over the notes to A, who then deposits them with his bank X, at more or less the same time that A is making the £100 payment to B. Alternatively, A could instruct his bank X to pay £100 to B's bank Y, and C could instruct her bank Y to pay £100 to A's bank X. The two banks would see that no movement – indeed, no handling – of notes was necessary at all. At bank X, individual A's account has received a £100 credit and made a £100 payment, and is therefore unchanged, while, at bank Y, B's account has risen by £100 and C's has fallen by the same amount. Transactions to the value of £200 have been carried out, but balance-sheet entries in the banking system have done all the work. Multiplying the £200 by a thousand, a million or a billion times does not affect the principle at work. More explicitly, by adding up all debits and credits for their customers, banks can dispense more or less entirely with the physical handling of notes, and so drastically reduce transactions costs.

But – in our example – what happens if C wanted to make a payment of £120 instead of £100 to A? In that case the business of bank Y's two customers (B and C) would result in instructions to pay £120 in notes and to receive £100, also in notes, so that bank Y must pay £20 in notes (net) over to bank X. The movement of £20 in notes between the two banks would be more economical than the movement of £220 in notes between the two banks and their three customers, but would still be a nuisance. The logical next stage in banking evolution was for a group of banks to form a clearing house, which they both capitalised (in order to pay for the building and infrastructure) and established as an entity where they would maintain deposits. To extend our example, the two banks X and Y know that occasional imbalances in their customers' debits and credits – such as the £20 imbalance referred to above – would occur from time to time, and so would credit, say, £50 *in notes* to the clearing house. The sum credited by a bank to the clearing house would be the maximum net debit (*in notes*, let it again be emphasised) it expected to arise from its customers' payment instructions, probably plus a small margin for safety. The beauty of the clearing-house arrangement is that, at the end of a particular day's business in which, say, bank Y had a net debit of £35, it does not even have to move notes to other banks, even though strictly its obligation is to pay in notes. Instead bank Y's balance at the clearing house would drop from £50 to £15. If the next day it received net credits of £35, its balance would return to £50. Vast volumes of business can be completed, without any resort to notes as such.

In the historical record the emergence of clearing houses was a gradual process. In England the process was driven by banks' clerks rather than by their proprietors: like so much else in the nitty-gritty of this subject, it was certainly not 'imposed from above'. According to Nevin and Davis's book on *The London Clearing Banks,*

> The first step towards establishing a regular system of clearance was taken by the 'walks' clerks themselves; some time around the mid-eighteenth century, they began to appreciate the advantages to themselves of meeting at a convenient place – usually a coffee house – and exchanging their drafts on each other, settling only the balance in cash. This informal and unauthorised exchange continued for some years until about 1770, when the practice of clearing was accorded official recognition by the private bankers of the City; in 1773 a room was hired for the purpose in the 'Five Bells', Dove Court, off Lombard Street.[3]

---

3   Edward Nevin and E. W. Davis, *The London Clearing Banks*, Elek, London, 1970, pp. 40–41.

Despite its rudimentary nature, the effect of an organised clearing was to economise on the volume of cash needed in settlement of a given turnover and so to lower the required ratio of cash to assets in banking institutions.

At this stage payment by means of cheques was unusual compared with other types of payment instruction, but over the next hundred years deposit banking via an extensive (and eventually national) branch network became the dominant form of banking business. Once a branch network and a national franchise had been established, payment by cheque took off. A related innovation facilitated these developments. As has been shown, banks could clear by the physical exchange of notes or across accounts in a clearing house. But clearing across accounts at the central bank, the bank which actually issues the notes, is even better. According to a volume issued on the tercentenary of the Bank of England:

> In 1854 joint stock banks in London joined the London
> Clearing House, and it was agreed that clearing by transfer
> of Bank of England notes would be abandoned in favour
> of cheques drawn on bank accounts held at the Bank. Ten
> years later the Bank of England itself entered the clearing
> arrangement, and cheques drawn on bankers' accounts at
> their Bank became considered as paid (i.e., cash).[4]

In late-nineteenth-century Britain most sizeable payments, and the overwhelming majority of transactions by value, were therefore made by cheque. The relevance of commercial banks' clearing arrangements to defining the Bank of England's role is of great importance and will be discussed in more detail shortly.

---

4   Forrest Capie et al. (eds), *The Future of Central Banking*, Cambridge University Press, Cambridge, 1994, p. 129.

But what happened in the USA, where the Federal Reserve did not exist until 1914?

Were the USA's clearing houses proto-central banks?

The USA has a federal system of government and is of course an enormous country in terms of its land area. Its constitution outlaws the private issue of the legal-tender coin, which is a power reserved to the federal government, but in the early nineteenth century thousands of banks issued notes. The notes circulated on the premise that, when presented to the issuing bank, they could be converted back into coin or 'specie' (i.e. gold or silver). The principle of clearing was well understood, but the multiplicity of note issues and the USA's geographical diversity resulted in a number of regional clearing houses, which contrasted with the undoubted leadership of London in England. A number of banks would participate, with the characteristic pattern being for banks to credit specie or (from 1865) national banknotes at one particular bank (a sort of regional 'central bank'). Inter-bank settlement took place via the resulting accounts at that bank. The celebrated Suffolk Bank system in New England, about which several academic articles have been written, was of this kind.[5]

From time to time confidence in the USA's banks would weaken and banks' note-holders would demand their specie back. Banks could meet these withdrawals either from their own vaults or by taking back some of the bullion left with the clearing-house association. The lower the level of their balance with the clearing

---

5   Donald J. Mullineaux, 'Competitive monies and the Suffolk Bank system: a contractual perspective', *Southern Economic Journal*, 53(4), 1987, pp. 884–98.

system (i.e., in fact, with the regional 'central bank'), the greater would be the likelihood that individual non-central banks would be overdrawn. (In our example, suppose bank Y's initial deposit with the clearing system was £30. If its customers instructed it to make net cash payments to other banks of £35, bank Y would have been overdrawn by £5.) So a financial crisis and the public's associated large-scale note redemptions would cause increased tension between members of the clearing house.

Although the USA had several large clearing houses, by the middle of the nineteenth century the New York Clearing House Association (NYCHA) was by far the largest and even acted as a kind of reserve clearing house to the regional clearing houses. In a major crisis in 1857 so-called 'country banks' were unable to meet their clearing obligations except by offering their own notes. In order to mitigate the shortage of true legal-tender cash, the NYCHA allowed its members to issue 'clearinghouse loan certificates' against the security of the country banks' notes. These loan certificates were a valid means of settling debts between the NYCHA's member banks. The rationale was that, because the NYCHA's members were confident of their own ultimate solvency, they could economise on specie by granting each other credit. The backing for the loan certificates was a stock of rather unreliable notes issued by the country banks, but – if over time debits and credits between clearing-house members netted out at a very low figure, and the country banks brought their affairs back into good order – that hardly mattered.[6]

Over the next few decades American clearing houses often

---

6   Richard H. Timberlake, 'The central banking role of clearinghouse associations', *Journal of Money, Credit and Banking*, 16(1), February 1984, pp. 1–15. See particularly pp. 3–4.

issued loan certificates in periods of strain, following the precedent set in 1857. In principle, they were to be called in once specie was again abundant and were viewed as a temporary expedient. But people – including ordinary citizens – regarded them as comparable to specie and they became widely used as a day-to-day currency. In two severe panics, in 1893 and 1907, they were regarded by many contemporaries as a clever expedient, which kept up the effective 'quantity of money' and so offset the deflationary effects of the hoarding of legal-tender coin and national banknotes. In 1907 the total of clearing-house certificates in issue peaked at $88.4 million, compared with the USA's estimated gross national product at the time of over $30 billion and a total of national banknotes outstanding of about $600 million.[7]

As noted by a textbook in the 1930s, the issue of clearing-house loan certificates in the crises of the late nineteenth century '... swept away the necessity of carrying extra till money' and 'by this means the member [of the clearing-house association] was better enabled to meet runs'.[8]

A plausible claim can be made that the USA's clearing houses were proto-central banks and, in that role, helped the banks to reduce the ratio of cash to assets. In the opening years of the twentieth century, however, American bankers and policymakers were unhappy about the performance of their monetary institutions. Although the clearing-house loan certificates facilitated payments and economised on cash, the truth was that the USA

---

7 The figure for clearing-house loan certificates comes ibid., p. 7. The other numbers are available in a variety of sources.

8 Ray B. Westerfield, *Money, Credit and Banking*, Ronald Press, New York, 1938, pp. 267–8.

lacked an 'elastic' note issue which could be quickly changed in response to banks' needs. American bankers also contrasted the enforced suspension of gold payments in their 1907 crisis with the contemporaneous success of the Bank of England in keeping the pound on the gold standard. Under legislation passed in 1908 a National Monetary Commission was established to investigate the monetary and banking institutions of other countries, and to make recommendations for the USA. The sequel to the commission's work was the establishment of a fully fledged central bank, the Federal Reserve, in 1914.

From Bagehot to Keynes

The flexibility of the US clearing houses in responding to cash runs was impressive and, from today's perspective, constitutes one of the best arguments that a government-sponsored central bank is not an inevitable feature of a modern economy. Nevertheless, the US banking industry did in the end favour their replacement by the kind of central banking arrangements already found in the UK and the rest of Europe. For the bankers it was the so-called 'inelasticity' of the USA's note issue which was its principal weakness. Whereas the Bank of England had a monopoly of the legal-tender note issue, and so could create notes quickly and readily, the US clearing houses could not do that.

The clearing houses did allow their members to operate with lower cash/asset ratios than would otherwise have been the case, but the US system was regarded as inferior to the English. In the late nineteenth century the leading members of the various clearing-house associations were supposed to be particularly solid representatives of US banking and so maintained a high ratio of cash reserves to deposit liabilities, often above 25 per cent.[9] But in England at the same time banks enjoying the advantages of limited liability, so-called 'joint-stock banks', were operating with cash/deposit ratios of under 10 per cent. In a letter from the governor of the Bank of England to the Chancellor of the Exchequer in the late 1850s, it was pointed out, 'The joint-stock banks of London, judging by their published accounts, have deposits to the amount of £30,000,000. Their capital is not more than £3,000,000, and they have on average £31,000,000 invested in one way or another, leaving only £2,000,000 as a reserve against all this mass of liabilities.'[10]

By implication, their cash/assets ratio was a mere 6 per cent, about a quarter that of similar institutions in the USA. In *Lombard Street*, Bagehot expressed misgivings about the very low ratio of cash to total assets, but fully appreciated the relationship between the banks' cash management practices and their profitability. In his words, 'If they had to keep a much larger part of their reserve in barren cash, their dividends would be reduced, and their present success would become less conspicuous.'[11]

The late nineteenth century saw the continued strengthening of the UK's joint-stock banks, as they perfected the system of inter-bank settlement in a central clearing house based in London

---

9   'Gillett (1900, pp. 203–4) compares reserve ratios of national banks in the United States to those of British joint-stock banks in the late nineteenth century. He finds reserve ratios of US national banks were more than double their British counterparts.' Charles W. Calomiris, *U S Bank Deregulation in Historical Perspective*, Cambridge University Press, Cambridge and New York, 2000, p. 40. See also Westerfield, op. cit., p. 184.

10   Walter Bagehot, *Lombard Street*, vol. IX in Norman St John-Stevas (ed.). *The Collected Works of Walter Bagehot*, The Economist, London, 1978 (originally published in 1873), p. 176.

11   Ibid., pp. 176–7.

and established national branch networks, often by amalgamation between regional banks. Following the Baring crisis of 1890, the joint-stock banks agreed to publish monthly statements in order that the public would be confident of the quality and safety of their business. An informal understanding was that they should keep their cash/asset ratio above 10 per cent, and in practice that meant a published figure of about 11 per cent. In reality the UK's joint-stock banks, now increasingly known as 'clearing banks', often operated with a somewhat lower ratio and dressed up their monthly numbers so that the published ratio was acceptable to their customers.

When Keynes wrote the newspaper articles that eventually appeared in his 1923 *Tract on Monetary Reform*, the number of London clearing banks had been much reduced by mergers and amalgamations. The five largest London clearing banks dominated English banking, and together with the two big Scottish banks (the Bank of Scotland and the Royal Bank of Scotland) they also dominated British banking. In Keynes's words, the Big Five banks' 'aggregate deposits have always been about nine times their "cash"'. Since the implied 11 per cent ratio is 'generally considered a "safe" proportion, it is bad for a bank's reputation to fall below it, while on the other hand it is bad for its earning power to rise above it'.[12] These arrangements continued with little change throughout the inter-war period, with Keynes giving a further, more detailed description in his 1930 *Treatise on Money*. While his treatments noted that to a large extent banks

---

12 John Maynard Keynes, *A Tract on Monetary Reform*, vol. IV in Donald Moggridge and Elizabeth Johnson (eds), *The Collected Writings of John Maynard Keynes*, Macmillan for the Royal Economic Society, London and Basingstoke, 1971 (originally published in 1923), p. 142.

operated with stable ratios because of their convenience as rules of thumb, both the *Tract on Monetary Reform* and the *Treatise on Money* alluded to the tension between the banking system's safety (increasing with the cash/assets ratio) and its profitability (decreasing with the cash/assets ratio). Keynes, like Bagehot, saw that any discussion of banking industry structure had to recognise that commercial banks were privately owned organisations with profit as one of their main objectives.

The ability to operate with an apparent cash ratio of 11 per cent, and a true cash ratio of 10 per cent or less, had been facilitated by two insights. The first was that the convertibility of deposits into cash could be protected by holding interest-bearing assets that could be readily sold for cash as well as by the holding of cash itself. The payment of interest on such 'liquid' assets helped profits, while their ready saleability for cash protected depositors. Second, if a distinct institution with the prerogative to issue notes (i.e. a central bank, which was the Bank of England in the UK's case) assumed a responsibility to lend to commercial banks if they ran out of cash, those banks could operate with lower cash/asset ratios than before.[13] Indeed, the key to maintaining deposit convertibility was not merely to have a large holding of idle vault cash, but also to nurture a good relationship with the Bank of England and keep holdings of an assortment of 'liquid assets'. It was understood that such assets could either be sold to the Bank or would serve as collateral for a loan. According to Nevis and Davis in their historical account in *The London Clearing Banks*, 'Improving communications and ready access to head

---

13   The assistance to the banking system might come in the form of purchases of securities, perhaps from strongly capitalised and liquid banks, and not just in the form of loans to banks. See Bagehot, op. cit., pp. 134–5.

offices, together with re-discounting facilities in the London bill market and the emergence of the Bank of England as "lender of last resort", had resulted in a tendency to work to a minimum of till money.'[14] Indeed, the British system of a small number of large clearing banks, with national branch networks and close connections with a central bank (i.e. the Bank of England) that would occasionally lend to them, 'was to serve as a model for monetary authorities throughout the world'.[15]

Trends in British banking in the second half of the twentieth century

Commercial banks' holdings of liquid assets other than cash improved the trade-off between profitability and depositor safety. For most of the twentieth century the Bank of England therefore paid close attention both to the clearing banks' cash ratio *and* to their 'liquidity ratio' (i.e. ratio of explicitly defined liquid assets to deposits held by non-banks). In the first few years after World War II the cash ratio dropped to 8 per cent, while the liquidity ratio was 40 per cent and banks' assets were dominated by claims on government. In such circumstances it was virtually inconceivable that a run would exhaust banks' cash holdings. A run might do serious damage to banks' initial cash holdings, but they could quickly sell some of their government securities to the Bank of England for cash, and so replenish the cash in their tills and vaults.

Over time the two ratios fell dramatically. By the late 1950s the Bank of England had allowed the liquidity ratio to go down to about 30 per cent, although the institutions specifically charged

---

14   Nevin and Davis, op. cit., p. 78.

15   Ibid., p. 82

with respecting this ratio – the clearing banks – resented the competition they faced from other credit-granting organisations not subject to ratio control. In the Competition and Credit Control reforms of 1971 the alleged discrimination against the clearers was largely remedied by the setting of a 'reserve assets ratio', applicable to all banks, at 12.5 per cent of sterling deposits. The clearers had to keep a non-interest-bearing balance at the Bank of England, equal to 1.5 per cent of deposits, on top of their required reserve assets, but this had an obvious functional rationale in their clearing activities and was not objectionable to them.

By now competition and risk-taking were intensifying, but British banking seemed still to be working smoothly. Although large-scale retail runs were mentioned in the history books, they no longer figured in the memory of anyone actually working in a British bank. In 1981 both the clearers' 1.5 per cent ratio and the 12.5 per cent reserve assets ratio were scrapped. Instead all banks – whether involved in clearing or not – were to lodge a deposit in 'special non-operational, non-interest-bearing accounts' at the Bank of England equal to 0.5 per cent of so-called 'eligible liabilities' (i.e. non-equity liabilities to agents other than banks and the government). Partly because of the fading collective memory of bank runs, these accounts were seen as serving no purpose in either monetary control or financial supervision and regulation. Instead they were understood to be a special mechanism, in effect a form of tax hypothecation, which gave the Bank of England funds to reinvest in interest-bearing securities and so to generate an income sufficient to cover its costs. The clearers kept a separate balance, over and above the 0.5 per cent, to settle debit and credit balances at the end of each daily clearing, but it was now a very low proportion of their balance sheet totals.

The Bank of England was still concerned about the degree of maturity transformation that the banks were undertaking. (Maturity transformation is the extending of long-term loans against short-term liabilities, including deposits repayable on demand.) The liquidity ratio was history and the reserve asset ratio had been abolished, but in July 1982 the Bank published a paper on 'The measurement of liquidity', showing how individual banks were to calculate (among other things) a 'net cumulative mismatched position'. Bank officials continued to supervise all banks' liquidity until 1998, when the job was transferred to the newly created Financial Services Authority as part of an institutional upheaval at the start of the Blair government. This institutional upheaval led to the transfer of many officials from the Bank of England, with its decades of experience and a fund of central banking know-how, to the FSA, which had yet to find its feet. Some officials at the FSA undoubtedly did appreciate that the structure of assets, and in particular the ratios of cash and liquidity to total assets, was relevant to the integrity of the banking businesses under its supervision. But a fair comment is that official interest in UK banks' ability to withstand a run was sharply less than had been the norm during the twentieth century.[16]

The insouciance towards banks' vulnerability in a run was

16 Several articles appeared in the Bank of England's *Financial Stability Review* between 2000 and 2005 on the UK banking system's liquidity. An article in the December 2000 issue (pp. 93–111), on 'Banking system liquidity: developments and issues', by Graeme Chaplin, Alison Emblow and Ian Michael, opined that 'the extent of maturity transformation at a three-month horizon in the UK banking system seems to be fairly stable through time'. A speech in November 2005 on 'Financial stability: managing liquidity risk in a global system' (pp. 78–84 in the December 2005 *FSR*) by Sir Andrew Large, then Deputy Governor for Financial Stability, correctly identified some of the problems that came out into the open less than two years later, but he left the Bank of England shortly afterwards.

reflected in several developments in the decade leading up to the Northern Rock crisis. Earlier discussion in this chapter established that banks' cash reserves with the Bank of England had a definite functional rationale for the depositing banks themselves. Their cash reserves were both the accounts in which the clearing banks themselves settled their end-of-day imbalances and a backstop for their vault cash, if their vault cash came under attack from a loss of confidence and a retail run. Further, by opening an account at the Bank of England a bank started a relationship with the UK's central bank, which included the possibility of borrowing from it in the appropriate circumstances. Some types of so-called 'bank' did not have an account at the Bank of England and could not appeal to it if they ran out of cash. Indeed, historically, building societies had not maintained accounts at the Bank of England. Instead they 'banked' via the clearing banks, while they had been regulated not by the Bank of England, but by the Registrar of Friendly Societies.[17]

But officialdom seems increasingly to have forgotten that banks' cash reserves at the Bank of England had an operational purpose. Under the terms of the 1998 Bank of England Act and the 2000 Financial Services and Markets Act, all UK 'banks' were required to maintain a non-interest-bearing balance at the Bank of England whether they undertook clearing and payments settlement business or not. Admittedly, the requirement was only 0.15 per cent of eligible liabilities and so was hardly a big threat to their profits. The Treasury subsequently published two consultative papers on what it had come to term 'the cash ratio deposit

---

17 Jack Revell, *The British Financial System*, Macmillan, London and Basingstoke, 1973, p. 367.

scheme'.[18] The scheme was discussed solely and entirely as a mechanism for covering the Bank of England's costs, and as having no wider value for the British banking system. The two documents seemed to be oblivious to the traditional rationale of a cash reserve at the central bank from the commercial banks' own point of view.

Before its demutualisation in October 1997, Northern Rock had been a mutually owned building society and its direct contacts with the Bank of England were perfunctory. Since 1998, like other British banks, it has kept a non-interest-bearing deposit at the Bank of England. In May 2006 the Bank of England changed the structure of its relationship with the UK's commercial banks in wide-ranging reforms, notably by starting to pay interest on cash reserves separate from the 0.15 per cent cash ratio deposit scheme. The new terms of the Bank of England's relationship with its customer banks were contained in a Red Book, which – in its own words – was 'designed to provide flexible access to central bank money, including in unlimited size against eligible collateral at a penalty rate through' the so-called 'standing lending facility'.[19]

---

18   The Treasury published two documents – both called *Review of the Cash Ratio Deposit Scheme: Consultation on proposed changes* – in August 2003 and August 2007. In qualification to the statement in the text, the Bank of England was fully aware of the significance of the cash ratio deposit scheme for banks' liquidity management. See *The Framework for the Bank of England's Operations in the Sterling Money Markets* ('the Red Book'), Bank of England, London, March 2008, p. 6.

19   'Red Book', p. 7. An important technical detail needs to be mentioned. Advances in computer technology enabled real-time gross settlement (RTGS) to be introduced for large sums in 1996. The change from the settlement of a balance at the end of the day (i.e. as in the daily cheque clearing) to RTGS enabled banks further to economise on cash. Some Bank of England officials have subsequently preferred the phrase 'settlement banks' to 'clearing banks', but 'clearing banks' remains the most common usage and has been retained here. The author understands that the RTGS equipment often broke down in the early years and more primitive systems had to be used as a back-up.

In the summer of 2007 Northern Rock was a participant in the Bank of England's reserve schemes and a member of the list of banks to which a standing facility might be granted. On the face of it, Northern Rock would have been behaving reasonably in expecting the Bank of England to be helpful, or at least 'flexible', if it had trouble financing its assets.

British banks' negligible cash holdings in the early 21st century

The events of August and September 2007 were to show that, in practice, no one in Northern Rock's management or the Bank of England knew precisely what was supposed to happen if Northern Rock lost the confidence of its retail depositors. Nevertheless, for most of Northern Rock's existence as a PLC the resilience of its defences against a retail run was not a big topic in its corporate strategy. Its regional roots and smallness handicapped it in the market for UK retail deposits. Here the clearers – with their national branch networks and the scale that allowed them to enjoy huge 'network economy' advantages in settlement business – were entrenched. But in truth, by the early 21st century the whole of the British banking system had economised on cash to a remarkable extent and, in this respect, taken a cavalier attitude towards funding risk. Cash as a fraction of total sterling liabilities, and even of sight sterling liabilities, had become nugatory by 2005. In January 2006 UK banks' cash ratio deposits were £1,953 million and other balances at the Bank of England (i.e. the balances actively used in settlement of payments business) were £839 million, and their vault cash was £5,417 million. Their total cash resources were therefore £8,209 million. At the same time

Figure 1 **Collapse in UK banks' cash/deposit ratio, 1960–2005**
Ratio of cash reserves to 'sight, time, savings and foreign
currency deposits' of UK banks, IMF data

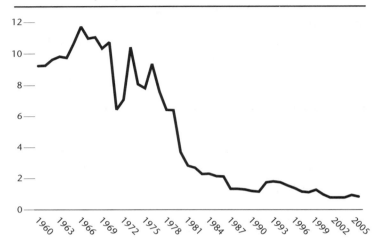

According to IMF data (which have the advantage of continuity over 45 years), the UK banks'
cash/deposits ratio fell from over 9% in 1960 to under 1% in 2005.
Source: IMF

their sight liabilities to UK non-banks were £629,892 million and
their total sterling liabilities £2,534,494 million. So the ratio of
cash to sight liabilities held 'by the British public' was 1.3 per cent
and the ratio of cash to all sterling liabilities was 0.3 per cent.[20] In
other words, the cash ratio of British banks had dropped to about
a thirtieth of what it had been 80 years earlier! Perhaps it is unnecessary to add that the situation in the summer of 2007 – which
had changed again because of the introduction of interest-earning

20 Figures are taken from relevant issues of *Financial Statistics*, The Stationery Office, London.

reserves in May 2006 – remained a far cry from the 100 per cent cash reserve ratio found when the idea of banking had been conceived in the late Middle Ages.

At any rate, the historical review over the last few pages has shown that British banking – which started, like all banking, with a cash/assets ratio of 100 per cent – was able to operate successfully for several years with a cash/assets ratio that was a fraction of 1 per cent. The spectacular reduction in banks' cash holdings had been made possible, among other things, by the help given by the Bank of England to Britain's banks in their balance sheet management. Critically, the Bank of England had been able and willing both to purchase a range of assets from them, and occasionally to lend to them, in order to relieve any cash shortages.

And what about banks in the USA and Europe?

Several books could be written about the cash-holding behaviour of the world's banking systems over the long run. There is room here only for a brief review of developments in the USA and Europe, in order to give a broader and more international perspective.

As explained above, from its inception one aim of the Federal Reserve System was to provide an elastic supply of cash to member banks and so lower US banks' cash/assets ratios. This was indeed an initial result of its creation. A contemporary US textbook on money and banking opined that 'as a constituent of our circulating media' the cash element (coins, government paper money and banknotes) was 'a small and declining proportion', and quoted a calculation by Angell and Ficek that cash had fallen from 18.1 per cent of the total circulating media in 1909 to 7.7 per cent

Figure 2 **US banks' cash/deposit ratios, 1934–2004**
% of deposit liabilities

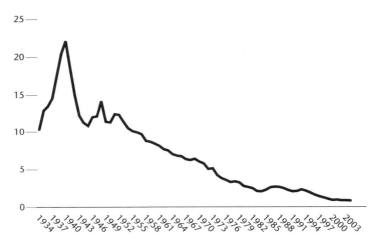

Source: Federal Deposit Insurance Corporation website

in 1930.[21] But the Great Depression of the early 1930s resulted in thousands of bank failures, and so caused both banks and people to hold more cash relative to their other assets. As a precaution against the return of troubled times, US banks' cash/deposits ratios were back above 20 per cent by the early 1940s. After World War II, however, banks worked together with the Federal Reserve to bring cash/deposits ratios down, with the results shown in Figure 2. The reduction in banks' cash/deposits ratios was helped by depositors' growing preference for time deposits, which by the 1980s paid an attractive interest rate. (Banks did not need to keep

---

21   Westerfield, op. cit., p. 184.

a cash reserve against time deposits, in contrast to sight deposits for which US officialdom had always demanded a cash reserve, both before and after the establishment of the Federal Reserve.) At any rate, by 2005 the ratio of cash to all deposits in US banking was under 1 per cent, not dissimilar to the figure in the UK.[22]

Until the introduction of the single European currency in 1999, the notion of a 'European banking system' was misplaced. The structures of banking systems varied from nation to nation and did not follow an exactly uniform pattern of development. Cash ratios took widely divergent values, with a compulsory cash ratio set well above banks' true functional needs in some countries.[23] When the euro was established on a scriptural basis in 1999, the European Central Bank began to pay interest on banks' cash reserves with it. This was a revolutionary innovation which – in one quantum leap – meant that Europe's banks were more favourably placed in their cash management arrangements than their counterparts in the USA or the UK. (Whether the payment of interest on reserves is good for the banking system's efficiency is a larger topic[24].) Apart from vault cash, banks in the newly formed single currency area had virtually no non-earning assets whatsoever. The same generalisation applies in the member states of the Eurozone as in the UK and the USA – that advances in central

---

22   Data are available from several websites, including those of the Federal Reserve and the Federal Deposit Insurance Corporation.

23   For example, Spain's banks in the 1980s were subject to a system of '*coeficientes*', required ratios of government debt to total assets. A senior banking executive is reported to have asked, 'Am I a banker at all? I am not allowed to be one.' T. Burns, 'Hamstrung by siphoning of deposits', *Financial Times*, 3 April 1985.

24   If interest is paid on banks' cash reserves at the central bank, they have less incentive to lend in the inter-bank market. Whether this affects the efficiency of the inter-bank market is moot, but see Tim Congdon and Brandon Davies, 'A simple plan to unclog the interbank market', *Financial Times*, 23 October 2008.

banking have helped banks to lower drastically the ratios of non-earning cash assets to total assets.

Long-run trends in bank solvency

For many decades, writers on monetary theory – and particularly writers on the theory of monetary policymaking – paid considerable attention to the ratios of cash and liquidity to banks' overall balance sheet size. By contrast, the ratio of capital to assets was neglected until the 1980s. One reason is that central banks did not always publicise their views on the desirable level of banks' capital/assets ratio. In the first edition of *The British Financial System*, published in 1973, Revell noted that building societies were subject to regulations on their capital reserves set by the Registrar of Friendly Societies, but for the banks matters were somewhat different. To quote, 'The Bank of England keeps a close watch on the reserve ratios of the bodies under its direct surveillance in the banking system – deposit banks, accepting houses, other secondary banks and discount houses. In all cases it works to certain minimum ratios, although nobody outside the Bank knows what these ratios are.'[25]

Of course, banks' management were cognisant of their capital ratios from internal records and they had to keep shareholders informed in their audited accounts. So – despite the apparent regulatory neglect of the capital side of banks' balance sheets until the last 25 years – researchers have been able to compile data on the long-run behaviour of capital ratios. As with the cash and liquidity ratios, the trend is clear. Whereas in the embryonic phase of banking capital/asset ratios put heavy emphasis on safety

---

25   Revell, op. cit., p. 105.

and were often over 30 per cent, in the twentieth century and the opening years of the 21st century the ratios fell substantially and with only occasional interruptions to the long-run pattern.[26]

This is not the place for a systematic treatment, but a summary verdict can be offered. (See Table 2 for relevant data.)[27] In the late nineteenth century a capital/assets ratio of over 15 per cent was normal even in the UK, the most advanced financial power of the time. By contrast, in the first half of the twentieth century the leading British banks regarded an appropriate capital/asset ratio as between 7 and 10 per cent. In the second half of the twentieth century the figure had fallen to 5 to 6 per cent. By the end of the century banks in the USA and Europe – which had historically operated on higher capital/asset ratios than their British counterparts – increasingly had the same attitude towards capital adequacy, but bank managements and regulators in these areas were dismayed by the very low capital/asset ratios in Japanese banking. Indeed, the view that the thinness of Japanese banks' capital cover allowed them to undercut their rivals in the offshore banking markets provoked the Anglo-American 'convergence accord' on bank capital in January 1987. The accord developed into the Basel capital rules, which were enforced in all the participating countries, including Japan, to establish a 'level playing field'. As is well known, the central principle of the first set of Basel guidelines was that capital should be not less than

---

26 The subject is of course vast, but – for example – see p. 124 of Howard Bodenhorn, *A History of Banking in Antebellum America*, Cambridge University Press, Cambridge, 2000. At end-June 1840 the Bank of Charleston had an equity-to-assets ratio of 60.6 per cent and a contingency fund of over 5 per cent of assets as well! It nevertheless earned a return on equity of about 10 per cent.

27 The data used in the table come from p. 149 of M. K. Lewis and K. T. Davis, *Domestic and International Banking*, Phillip Allan, Oxford, 1987.

8 per cent of assets, with equity capital equal to at least half of total capital. The similarity of this principle to the capital/assets ratio of about 5 per cent preferred by Britain's banks is striking. Given the pattern of the preceding international negotiations in which UK officials had been so active, the setting of a 4 per cent minimum may not have been entirely accidental.

Table 2 **Equity capital to total assets of UK and US banks, 1880–1985**

	UK banks*	US banks†
1880	16.8	n/a
1900	12.0	n/a
1914	8.7	18.3
1930	7.2	14.2
1940	5.2	9.1
1950	2.7	6.7
1966	5.3	7.8
1980	5.9	6.8
1985	4.6	6.9

*UK deposit banks 1880–1966, UK clearing bank groups 1980 and 1985
†All member banks of the Federal Reserve system
The low value of the UK ratio in 1950 reflected the high ratio of low-risk government paper in banks' assets after World War II.
Source: See note 27

Like all other British banks, Northern Rock was subject to the Basel rules at its demutualisation. Indeed, references to compliance with the latest developments in the Basel regulatory framework were included in its last published accounts as a quoted PLC, only a few weeks before its collapse.[28] Perhaps it is premature to

---

28 Also neglected – as mentioned in the text – are the complications arising from banks' issue of bonds and reference capital. Liabilities are deemed, for simplicity, to consist solely of equity capital and deposits.

pass judgement on international banks' manipulation of asset and liability structures over the last decade or so, as they attempted to bypass the Basel constraints by the creation of artificial 'special purpose vehicles' or 'conduits'. Nevertheless, even a cursory examination of banks' annual reports shows that in the last few years actual ratios of equity capital to assets have often been under 3 per cent for a very large number of institutions. They nevertheless met the Basel rules because those rules allow a zero weight (in terms of capital usage) for inter-bank exposures and claims on government, as well as other technical exemptions.

To conclude this section, in the early phase of modern industrialism banks typically had capital/asset ratios of over 30 per cent, but in the middle years of the present decade the 'average' ratio of equity capital to assets (if the phrase has any definite meaning) may have been about 5 per cent and the effective ratio for a surprisingly high number of prominent institutions was little more than 3 per cent.

What do the trends in liquidity and solvency imply for loan margins?

It is now time to bring together the strands of the argument by setting out a table which shows how, for a particular target return on equity, the average return on bank assets varies with different ratios of cash and capital to assets. Table 3 uses the formula developed at the end of Chapter 2 for the determination of banks' average return on assets. A reminder may usefully be inserted that the implicit assumptions in preparing the matrix are the same as they have been throughout this paper, that banks have no loan losses, and that their fee revenues cover the costs of organising the loans, and of running any deposit collection and money transmission infrastructure.

A target rate of return on capital of 14 per cent has been chosen, as this sort of number would be regarded as appropriate by contemporary UK banks in their internal strategy documents and serves as a reasonable benchmark for discussion.[29] In the very early days of banking – when banking was indeed little different from risky and avaricious moneylending, and the cash ratio was perhaps 80 per cent and the capital/assets ratio 45 per cent – the loan margin had to exceed 30 per cent. In the opening decades of the Industrial Revolution, in such countries as England, Scotland and the USA, a cash ratio of 40 per cent and a capital/asset ratio of 20 per cent would have been commonplace in the banking industry. A loan margin of almost 5 per cent (i.e. 500 basis points) would achieve a return on capital of 14 per cent. In the early decades of the post-war world, with a cash ratio of 5 per cent and a capital/assets ratio of 8 per cent, a loan margin of about 200 basis points would have been consistent with that return on capital. But in the low-ratio banking of the last fifteen years or so, loan margins of 100 basis points or less were compatible – assuming all went well with asset selection and cost control – with high bank profitability.

---

29 Northern Rock was one of several British banks to have exceeded the 14 per cent figure by a wide margin for many years, until its funding – and so the business itself – collapsed in late 2007. The chief economic commentator of the *Financial Times*, Martin Wolf, protested about the high profitability of banking in a column on 28 November 2007, attributing it to 'sundry explicit and implicit guarantees' from the state. Later in his column he endorsed 'higher capital requirements' for banks.

Table 3 **How banks' loan margins vary with their cash and solvency ratios**

The table shows, with a given target rate of return on capital, how a reduction in banks' average return on assets (i.e. their 'loan margin', more or less) becomes possible as their cash/asset and capita/asset ratios decline. All figures are expressed as a percentage.

P/K Rate of return on capital	C Cash ratio	K/A Capital/assets ratio	r_b 'Loan margin'
14	80	45	31.5
14	40	20	4.7
14	12	15	2.4
14	5	8	2.2
14	1	5	0.8
14	1	3	0.5

4 THE SOCIAL COSTS AND BENEFITS OF CENTRAL BANKING

The usual context of the phrase 'social cost–benefit analysis' is the appraisal of major public sector investment projects, with the aim of the analysis being to see how the value of a project's output to society compares with its resource cost. To adopt the phrase in a discussion of the structure of banking systems may seem odd. Central banks are, however, found almost universally in present-day market economies. Why? What are the benefits to the economy at large that justify their staff costs and rents (and indeed, in the case of the Bank of England, quite a lot of flummery and tinsel)?

Two types of benefit are particularly important. The first is a reduction in the cost of bank finance, the explanation for which arises from the material in the last two chapters; the second is an increase in the flexibility of bank finance, which requires a new line of analysis to be developed in this chapter.

Lower costs of bank finance

Chapter 3 demonstrated that banks had lowered their cash/asset ratios and capital/asset ratios drastically since they first evolved from primitive moneylending, and that these long-run patterns owed much to the innovation of central banking. The driver was profit maximisation. The algebraic argument at the end of

Chapter 2 showed that, for any particular loan margin, the rate of return on banks' capital increases as the cash/asset and capital/asset ratios decline. Privately owned banks valued the services provided to them by central banks, since these services enabled them – with unchanged risk – to raise the ratio of earning assets to total assets and to increase their leverage. With a given level of equity, the result of increased earning assets and more leverage was higher profits.

But how do higher profits for bankers translate into benefits for society? It must be remembered that unusually high profitability in banking ought to induce the entry of new capital and the intensification of competition. As Alfred Marshall elaborated in Book VI of his 1890 classic, *Principles of Economics*, in the long run the rate of return on capital ought to be the same in all industries. The supply price of banking services – which here means 'the loan margin' – ought to come down until banks' revenues exceed costs only by enough to deliver a 'normal' rate of return. The various innovations considered in Chapter 3 – such as the setting-up of clearing houses and the establishment of central banks – initially cut banks' cash and capital ratios, and helped their profits. But over time they caused banks to offer loan facilities at a lower interest rate to non-banks. Central banking therefore lowered the cost of bank finance throughout the economy.

The discussion can now be readily linked to the formal concepts of theoretical welfare economics. Given a society's production possibilities, a function relating the marginal return on capital to the size of the capital stock can be proposed (see Figure 3). In the absence of a central bank, banks' loan margins have to compensate for the risk of bank runs and the associated potential illiquidity, and so the effective rate of interest in investment

Figure 3   **Banks' loan margins and output per worker
(i.e. living standards)**

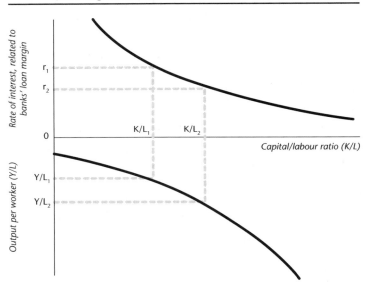

As banks' loan margins fall, the rate of interest in investment decisions drops from r_1 to r_2, the capital/labour ratio rises from K/L_1 to K/L_2 and output per worker increases from Y/L_1 to Y/L_2.

decisions is r_1. Once central banks have emerged, banks have lower cash/asset ratios and lower margins, and the rate of interest falls to r_2 and the equilibrium capital stock increases. Assuming that the society has a conventional production function, the rise in the capital stock ought to be associated with rises in the capital/labour ratio and the marginal productivity of labour. Again, assuming the usual relationships of neoclassical economics, a rise in the marginal productivity of labour ought to be accompanied by higher wages and living standards.

The effects of reductions in banks' cash/asset and capital/

asset ratios on loan margins can, for any given rate of return on capital, be calculated using the formula given in Chapter 2. Whereas Table 3 at the end of the last chapter included a target rate of return on capital of 14 per cent, since that would be a challenge in the long run, Table 4 below uses a target rate of return of 7 per cent. The experience of market capitalism seems to be that the long-run rate of return on equity investment is around the level of about 6 to 7 per cent a year, according to most studies that have considered the subject.[1]

Table 4 **How banks' loan margins vary with their cash ratios**

The table shows how, with a given target rate of return on capital and capital/assets ratio, a reduction in banks' average return on their earning assets (i.e. their loan margin, more or less) becomes possible as the cash ratio falls. All figures expressed as a percentage.

P/K Rate of return on capital	C Cash ratio	K/A Capital/assets ratio	r_b 'Loan margin'
7	80	5	1.7
7	60	5	0.8
7	40	5	0.5
7	20	5	0.4
7	5	5	0.3
7	1	5	0.3

One point suggested by the table is that the big gains in banking efficiency came before central banking. The historical record suggests banks had cut their cash/asset ratios to the 20–30 per cent area before a distinct central bank was split from the rest

---

1   See, for example, Elroy Dimpson, *The Triumph of the Optimists*, University Presses of California, Columbia and Princeton, 2002.

of the banking industry. The table shows that – on the assumptions (i.e. a 7 per cent rate of return on capital and a capital/assets ratio of 5 per cent) – a fall in the cash/asset ratio from 20 per cent to 1 per cent leads to a narrowing of loan margins only from 44 basis points to 35 basis points. Nevertheless, this is a gain worth having.

Table 5 **How banks' loan margins vary with their capital/asset ratios**

The table shows how, with a given target rate of return on capital and cash ratios, a reduction in banks' average return on their earning assets becomes possible as the capital/assets ratio falls. All figures are expressed as a percentage.

P/K Rate of return on capital	C Cash ratio	K/A Capital/assets ratio	r_b 'Loan margin'
7	1	45	3.18
7	1	20	1.41
7	1	15	1.06
7	1	8	0.57
7	1	5	0.35
7	1	3	0.21

The position is rather different with the capital/assets ratio. The introduction of central banking, and the associated improvements in banking regulation and supervision, ought to allow a reduction in capital/assets ratios. Table 5 shows that reductions in capital/asset ratios have a major effect on acceptable loan margins, even when the capital/assets ratio is already quite modest. A return on assets of just 60 basis points results in a reasonable return on capital when the capital/assets ratio is 8 per cent, but a return on assets as meagre as 20 basis points has the same outcome when the capital/assets ratio is 3 per cent. Spreads as low as this have been found only in international whole-sale banking, notably in the so-called 'euro-markets' centred in London. The relevance of the capital requirement to the conduct of business, and the battle for market share, is obvious. No wonder that American and European banks resented the competition from Japanese rivals in these markets in the 1980s given that the Japanese operated with markedly lower capital/asset ratios.

More flexible lending facilities

The historical record shows that credit preceded banking. Inscriptions on clay tablets show that loans were being made between merchants in the ancient Near East (modern Iraq and Syria) over four thousand years ago, well before the start of banking. In the pre-banking era a loan by one merchant to another required that the lender reduce his stock of the loan material, often a precious metal, in order to acquire a claim on the borrower. A loan could not be made before the creditor's prior holding of the asset that he or she was to lend. This is a far from silly way of looking at credit arrangements in the modern world. Some people may believe that, when they are granted a bank loan, the loan comes out of a big pot of banknotes which has had a prior existence over an extended period. Isn't it common sense to think that the bank – like the merchant in ancient history – cannot lend unless it already holds the requisite number of banknotes? After all, money doesn't grow on trees, does it?

In fact, banking practice is epitomised when both loan proceeds and bank deposits are created out of thin air. Unlike the merchant in ancient history, a bank does not need to hold in advance the physical substance – the legal-tender notes – that constitute the material which makes up its loans. The ability to conjure up new money from nothing may seem to be magic, and this characteristic of banking undoubtedly baffles and surprises many people. But there is no magic involved. When a bank extends a new loan, it adds by 'a stroke of the pen' identical sums to its assets (its loan portfolio) and its liabilities (its deposits). The extra assets and liabilities cancel out. Its own net worth – its equity capital – is unchanged. If borrowers were all immediately to ask for loan proceeds to be converted into cash, the bank's cash holding could be threatened and might even run out. (The bank would still have assets in the form of loans.) But in practice borrowers are no more likely to want to convert a new deposit (i.e. a deposit created by a loan) into cash than are depositors in general. Typically a borrower intends to use the proceeds to purchase an asset and the purchase is made by a payment instruction from one bank to another. Bank loans lead to payments between banks, with debits and credits largely cancelled in the clearing process. In the normal course of events little or no cash leaves the banking system.

Banks' ability to add identical amounts to loan assets and deposit liabilities, and so to create new money from scratch, facilitates a particularly useful type of product, the overdraft. A standard overdraft facility specifies a maximum borrowing figure, but no minimum, giving the borrower discretion about the size of his loan. Loan principals can be borrowed and repaid several times in a year, if that suits the bank's customers. Some types of business – with dealers in financial securities and commodities being the best examples – have large and unpredictable balance sheets. When trading opportunities arise, the drawing-down of the overdraft allows them to own 'books' of securities and commodities (and make a trading turn on them) which are many times their own capital. On the other hand, when business is quiet and their own 'books' are the same or lower than their capital, they can repay the overdraft and they have no interest charges to cover.

Two types of loan facility can be compared, the overdraft facility and a fixed-sum, fixed-period loan. If only the fixed-sum, fixed-period loan were available, dealers in financial securities and commodities would have either to limit their 'book' to their own capital or to guess in advance the maximum book that would be profitable and borrow an amount equal to the excess of that over their capital. The result would be an obvious loss of flexibility relative to the overdraft method of finance. With an overdraft the average size of a dealer's loan is equal to the average size of the book (minus capital), not the maximum size, in a particular period. Interest costs are clearly reduced, while the risk of misjudging the opportunities available (i.e. of taking out a costly fixed-sum and fixed-period loan ahead of a quiet trading period) does not arise. In the first instance the availability of overdrafts ought therefore to boost the profitability of trading in securities and commodities. The gains ought, however, eventually to spread more widely. Commodity dealers supply wholesalers and wholesalers supply retailers. If the provision of overdraft finance by banks is accompanied by competition, commodity dealers' lower interest costs should lead to a narrowing of the margins they charge to wholesalers and, eventually, to lower prices in the shops. More generally, banking and other forms of financial intermediation give business more choice about when to open and close financial exposures of various kinds, and – if the system is running well – this expansion of opportunities costs next to nothing in resource terms.

In view of the benefits of overdrafts to the economy, it must be socially advantageous if the banking industry is structured so that it can provide them. But let us now return to the discussion of banks' ability to create credit and money by a stroke of the pen. Crucial to that process is that, when a bank (say Bank Alpha) adds a sum to its borrowing customer's deposit, the customer does not immediately convert the loan proceeds into cash. Instead the customer buys an asset by making a payment to another individual, perhaps a customer of another bank (Bank Beta). If a large number of Bank Alpha's customers take up overdraft facilities at the same time and all make payments to Bank Beta, Bank Gamma and Bank Delta, then Bank Alpha may have to transfer cash to these other banks in excess of its own original cash holding, leading to a crisis. (The logic here is just the same as in the discussion of clearing in Chapter 3. Remember that non-banks settle their accounts at banks; banks settle in cash, i.e. notes or their balance at the central bank.) Fortunately, each bank is only part of the larger system. For most of the time the customers of Banks Beta, Gamma and Delta draw down their overdrafts at roughly the same rate, relative to their agreed maximum facilities, and also to the banks' total assets and capital, as those of Bank Alpha. The existence of overdraft arrangements should not lead to recurrent crises in the clearing system.

But banks must take precautions. Bank Alpha may be very well capitalised, and prudent and careful in the conduct of its business. Nevertheless, it may – for reasons that it could not have foreseen – experience very heavy drawing-down of overdrafts by its customers, relative to the rest of the banking industry. So its vault cash and central bank balance are depleted, and it may be in danger of being unable to repay deposits with notes. Of course, it ought to have liquid securities that it can sell quickly to replenish its cash, but suppose – again for reasons that it could not have foreseen – that the market in such securities is closed. The only remaining potential supplier of legal-tender cash is the institution that issues the legal tender, namely the central bank. In summary, Bank Alpha is more willing to offer overdraft facilities to its non-bank customers, with all the wider benefits throughout the economy, if the central bank is prepared to lend to it in an emergency. More generally, the flexibility of the commercial banks' lending arrangements is enhanced by the central bank's acceptance of a lender-of-last-resort role. The banking system best serves the interests of non-banks throughout the economy when, in turn, the central bank serves the interests of the banking system by extending loans when its members are short of cash.

Central banking has large net social benefits

Chapter 2 concluded that 'bankers are likely to support any developments, in technology or institutions, including the institutional relationships within their own industry, which enable them to lower their cash/deposits ratio (i.e. their "liquidity") and their capital/assets ratio (i.e. their "solvency")'. Chapter 3 demonstrated that central banking – along with other innovations, particularly in the technology of payments settlement – had led to large falls in banks' cash/deposits ratio and capital/assets ratio over the centuries, but particularly in the 150 years or so since the 1860s, when the modern concept of a 'central bank' first became viable and Bagehot began to theorise about it. So there can be no surprise that commercial bankers favour the establishment of central banks. But this chapter has established that, while the benefits of central banking may initially accrue to banks' managements and shareholders, in the long run the benefits are diffused throughout the economy. Falls in banks' cash/asset and capital/asset ratios lead to a decline in banks' loan margins, and narrower loan margins imply a reduction in financing costs throughout business, a larger capital stock and higher living standards. In addition, when commercial banks are able to bolster cash by ready sales of securities to the central bank or even by borrowing from it, they are more prepared to extend overdraft facilities to their customers. Initially the widespread availability of overdrafts helps the profits of dealers in securities and commodities, but ultimately competition narrows dealing spreads and reduces costs to the retail customer. So – to put the matter crudely and succinctly – central banking makes people better off.[2]

A rigorous demonstration that these benefits exceed the costs of central banking will not be attempted here. But it is evident that the effects of central banking on the cost and quality of the services that banks provide to non-banks are positive. By contrast, the resource cost of central banking is negligible. In general the central bank needs to transact on a regular basis only with banking organisations heavily involved in cheque clearing and payments settlement, and these organisations tend to be large and few in number because their distinctive activities are characterised by pronounced 'network economies'.[3] The average unit size

2   The innovation of central banking ought to raise the ratio of bank assets and liabilities to GDP. The argument that the real capital stock is a positive function of the ratio of bank assets and liabilities to GDP is contained in Ronald I. McKinnon, *Money and Capital in Economic Development* , Brookings Institution, Washington, DC, 1973, notably in Chapter 9.

3   The importance of network economies in clearing business is part of the

of transactions between central banks and commercial banks is enormous (running in the UK's case to many millions of pounds), while credit assessment can be high level and related exclusively to the banking sector rather than being micro-managed at the level of small loans to non-banks. An institution like a central bank has a small cost (in terms of staff, buildings and so on) and a large public benefit. But – in order to deliver its substantial net social benefit – a central bank must be able to lend money to banks. The central bank must be a lender of last resort, as hundreds of text-books have said.[4]

For all the brickbats thrown at 'bankers', their bonuses, 'Wall Street', 'The City of London' and so on, it cannot be denied that across the industrial world recent decades have seen narrower loan margins, finer spreads in securities and commodities trading, greater diversity in financing options for companies, and increasingly capital-intensive production. Those cynical about market capitalism may mock these advantages, but they are real and important. Is it necessary to recall that communism broke down less than twenty years ago? One of the salient aspects of the transition to market economies in central and eastern Europe from 1990 was the development of profit-motivated commercial banks and the separation of such banks from a central bank with the usual recognised functions. Mono-banking (i.e. the extension of credit from a single banking institution rather than a number of competing institutions) and central planning were hopelessly

---

explanation for the relatively small number of large clearing banks in most countries and often gives rise to competition concerns.

4   In a celebrated 1987 article Goodhart proposed a somewhat different rationale for central banking from that set out in Chapters 3 and 4 of this study. See Charles Goodhart, 'Why do banks need a central bank?', *Oxford Economic Papers*, 39, Oxford University Press, Oxford, 1987, pp. 75–89.

inefficient at allocating resources, when compared with the highly competitive financial systems of market economies, and the dichotomisation between commercial and central banking which characterises them. We have shown how a central bank not only brings value to the economy in general but that it arises, perhaps not surprisingly given its important functions, as a spontaneous product of market forces in banking. This clearly contrasts not only with the former communist economies, but also with the 'free banking' view that a central bank should be prevented from emerging.

What about the flummery and tinsel? Is it necessary at the beginning of the 21st century for visitors to the Bank of England to be met by gentlemen wearing pink tunics and top hats? In strict functional terms, of course, it is not. The fancy dress does, however, serve the purpose of warning people that the central bank is different from other types of bank. Because no other bank can issue legal-tender banknotes, the Bank of England has been uniquely well equipped to act as go-between in inter-bank transactions, honest broker in banking mergers and arbiter in occasional disputes. Reminders that the Bank has a distinguished history are more than merely decorative.

5 THE LENDER-OF-LAST-RESORT ROLE

The last chapter established that, if a central bank is to deliver the substantial benefits that it can potentially make to economic efficiency and social welfare, it must be a lender of last resort. In a modern economy the state has granted the central bank the exclusive right to issue legal-tender notes. The central bank is therefore distinct from the rest of the banking system because it alone has the power to make loans to private sector agents in such notes (i.e. the ultimate 'cash' of business and finance, and the money with which banks settle between themselves). The argument here has been that it must be prepared to use that power in certain circumstances. But to which agents should the central bank extend loans, what are the circumstances that justify lender-of-last-resort activity, and on what terms should lender-of-last-resort loans be made?

First-resort and last-resort loans

Before answering these questions, a warning has to be given and a distinction is to be drawn between two kinds of central bank facility.[1] The warning is that in the next few sections it is implicit

---

1   Note that loan facilities are not the only way that a central bank interacts with commercial banks. As Chapter 7 explains, central banks sometimes purchase assets outright from commercial banks. They can also extend guarantees to a lending bank in the inter-bank market.

(unless made explicit) that central bank loans are to solvent banks – that is, banks that have an excess of assets over non-equity liabilities. The assumption is dropped in the penultimate section, which considers whether the central bank should lend to an institution that is known to be insolvent. A final section discusses the advisability of the nationalisation of troubled banks in a free-market economy.

What about the two kinds of central bank facility? The first kind is intended to implement monetary policy decisions and sets the rate of interest in the short-term money markets. Typically, the central bank buys interest-bearing securities from a commercial bank and arranges that the commercial bank will repurchase the security at a different, lower price at an agreed future date. The difference between the price at which the commercial bank sells to and repurchases from the central bank implies an interest rate on the transaction. By varying the so-called 'repurchase rate' in this way, the central bank determines interest rates.[2] Various features of such repurchase (or repo) transactions are worth mentioning. In particular, because the commercial bank has agreed to buy back the securities in question, a default risk arises for the central bank only if both the issuer of the security and the repo-ing bank fail during the period of the repurchase agreement. This risk is usually negligible, even if the issuer is in the private sector. Further, since a repurchase date is specified, the agreement has a clear and definite life.

Alternatively, a commercial bank facing a temporary cash

---

2   Although the phrase 'repo rate' is often equated with the central bank's desired policy rate, the central bank could determine the short-term interest rate by other means – for example, outright purchases and sales of Treasury bills. Indeed, until ten or fifteen years or so ago such outright transactions were more common in British central banking than repurchase activity.

shortfall may borrow against the collateral of securities that might otherwise have been sold to and repo-ed from the central bank. Assuming that the securities are of the same quality, and that a date is set for repayment and honoured, the economic substance of the loan is the same as that of a repurchase agreement. A loan of this sort – with limited risk to both parties and a well-defined terminal date, and priced with a monetary policy purpose – might be termed a 'first-resort loan'.[3] The purchase and sale of securities on repo terms, and central bank loans with the same economic substance, are often called 'open market operations'.

The second kind of facility is different in several respects. If a bank sells securities to the central bank or takes out a loan on first-resort terms, it does have a cash shortfall that needs to be bridged, but it is implicit that the cash shortfall is technical, transient and unimportant. From time to time, however, banks run into more serious cash trouble. They may have an ample cushion of equity capital, and their assets may be loans and securities that are almost certain eventually to be paid back in full. Nevertheless, they may suffer recurrent cash deficits when they settle business at the end of the day with other banks and/or have insufficient cash in their branch networks. When they ask the central bank for a loan, it is because other financing options have dried up. Because they cannot predict exactly when their cash problem will be resolved, they borrow from the central bank without any definite repayment date.[4] They ought to offer – and normally do offer –

---

3   The description of routine Bank of England transactions as 'first-resort' in nature was made by the influential City monetary commentator Gordon Pepper, on a number of occasions. See, for example, pp. 67–8 of Gordon Pepper and Michael Oliver, *Monetarism under Thatcher*, Edward Elgar, Cheltenham, UK, and Northampton, USA, 2001.

4   On 18 November 1993 the then governor of the Bank of England, Edward George

satisfactory collateral to the central bank for the help they are receiving. But they cannot make a binding contractual commitment as to how exactly they will repay the loan. In contrast with the repurchase agreements usually found in standard, run-of-the-mill open-market operations, the central bank faces uncertainty about when and even whether the loan will be repaid. Nevertheless, if the collateral is of acceptable quality, its ultimate default risk ought to be insignificant.

It is this second kind of facility which is known as a 'lender-of-last-resort loan'. In general, open-market operations and first-resort loans are relevant to the setting of interest rates and the central bank's first objective of achieving monetary stability, while lender-of-last-resort loans arise when part or all of the banking system has a deep-seated cash problem. Lender-of-last-resort facilities are intended to promote the second objective of financial stability.[5] Further, whereas open-market operations tend to be initiated by the central bank, it is generally a commercial bank with a cash problem which opens the negotiations with the central bank for a lender-of-last-resort loan.

(now Lord George), gave a lecture at the London School of Economics on the principles of last-resort lending. He said that, when making a last-resort loan, the Bank looks 'for a clear exit'. George, 'The pursuit of financial stability', *Bank of England Quarterly Bulletin*, 43(1), Bank of England, London, February 1994, p. 65.

5   Note that in practice the distinction between first-resort and last-resort loans can be blurred. After the breakdown of the international wholesale and inter-bank markets in the summer of 2007, the Bank of Spain extended three-month facilities to Spanish banks and these could be deemed as for monetary policy purposes. But it seems likely that in some cases the three-month loans were renewed at least twice, so that the facilities were in effect last-resort in nature. Central bank funding replaced market funding, with the objective of maintaining financial stability. The author discussed this in his 2008 pamphlet *Northern Rock and the European Union*, Global Vision, London, pp. 11–13.

Which organisations should qualify for lender-of-last-resort loans?

The first discussion point is to determine which organisations qualify for lender-of-last-resort facilities. We may recall that financial stability is about maintaining the full convertibility of bank deposits into notes. In most financial systems a commitment to maintain such convertibility is offered by certain types of institution that take deposits, but are not involved in cheque clearing or payment settlement. They repay cash over the counter, but do not hand out chequebooks. Traditional examples in Britain included the building societies and the trustee savings banks. They can make payments by cheque only because they, like non-banks, keep accounts at a second and different kind of bank, the banks that do offer cheque clearing and money transmission services. As noted in Chapter 3, in the UK context banks of this second sort are commonly called 'clearing banks'.[6]

Moreover, clearing banks have long had accounts at the Bank of England, because – again as explained in Chapter 3 – settlement of inter-bank balances is much easier across such accounts than by the physical movement of notes. Although Bank of England officials may deny that keeping these accounts gives the clearing banks automatic entitlement to a loan of any description, a fair comment is that any bank – even a central bank – will readily lend only to customers with which it is familiar. By opening an account with the Bank of England, a bank starts a business relationship with the central bank. To that extent it takes the first steps in qualifying for a loan facility, including a last-resort loan.

---

6   As mentioned in note 19 to Chapter 3, some Bank of England officials prefer the phrase 'settlement banks' to 'clearing banks', but 'clearing banks' remains the dominant usage.

In practice the Bank of England and all other central banks see banks that take retail deposits, and hence are involved in the payments mechanism, as prime candidates for lender-of-last-resort loans in a crisis. As early as 1873, when he published *Lombard Street*, Bagehot had seen that 'no cause is more capable of producing a panic ... as the failure of a first rate joint stock bank in London'.[7] In 1930 the Bank of England incurred a heavy loss in the covert rescue of a minor clearing bank, Williams Deacon, in order that its difficulties could be kept out of the public eye. The Bank felt that it had 'to save the face of British banking'. The Bank's loss, which fell on its private shareholders, was just under 0.1 per cent of GDP, which would today (November 2008) be about £1.1 billion.[8] Precisely because clearing banks are important to the payments mechanism and confidence in them must be preserved, the normal pattern has been that they are subject to tighter balance-sheet supervision than non-clearing banks. The clearing banks' resentment of the weight of regulation in the 1950s and 1960s, including the high cash and liquidity ratios of that era, was one of the pressures behind the reduction in these ratios that occurred in later decades and was chronicled in Chapter 3.

In normal conditions the central bank is far more reluctant to lend to non-clearing banks than to clearing banks. Non-clearing banks are a motley bunch, with marked differences in their asset composition and funding patterns. Thus, virtually all the loan assets of building societies and specialist mortgage lenders are

---

7   Walter Bagehot, *Lombard Street*, vol. IX in Norman St John-Stevas (ed.), *The Collected Works of Walter Bagehot*, The Economist, London, 1978 (originally published in 1873), p. 182.

8   Richard Sayers, *The Bank of England 1891–1944*, Cambridge University Press, Cambridge, 1976, pp. 127–33.

residential mortgages, whereas 'industrial banks' make loans only to companies. (The UK has not had many specialist industrial banks, although they have featured prominently in the financial history of, for example, Japan and France.) It was mentioned in Chapter 3 that the Bank of England had no historical connections with the building societies and would not have been expected to lend to them if they ran into cash difficulties. The central bank cannot, however, be indifferent to failures in any part of the financial system, since losses in a low-grade, peripheral business may ricochet around the banks and hit confidence. As events since August 2007 illustrate, paralysis in the inter-bank market can impair the ability even of soundly run banks to finance their assets. Rather than make a loan itself, the central bank may persuade well-regulated and highly capitalised banks with which it has close relations to make loans to troubled institutions. That was the approach adopted by the Bank of England in the secondary banking crisis of 1974–76. A concerted programme of inter-bank lending (known as 'the lifeboat') enabled recently created secondary banks to shed loss-making property loans grad- ually. If the lifeboat had not been launched, the secondary banks would have been forced to call in property loans and property assets would have been sold in a rush, causing even larger falls in values than in fact took place.[9]

Are there any occasions on which the central bank ought to lend to non-banks or, at any rate, to organisations calling them- selves banks which do not take deposits? In the recent crisis the Federal Reserve made large loans to J. P. Morgan to help it acquire Bear Sterns, one of the USA's most prominent financial

---

9   The classic account is Margaret Reid, *The Secondary Banking Crisis 1973–5: Its Causes and Course*, Macmillan, London, 1982.

companies, and to AIG, the world's largest insurance company. Bear Sterns did not take deposits and was not a member bank of the Federal Reserve System. It was, above all, a company that traded and underwrote securities. It offered, however, global clearing services to broker dealers, prime broker clients (mostly hedge funds) and other professional traders, and was particularly important for the clearing of derivative trades. The Federal Reserve was worried that the failure of Bear Sterns would lead to the disruption of these clearing arrangements, with knock-on effects to other payment clearing systems. So – although Bear Sterns was not a bank – its operations were relevant, if at a few removes, to the convertibility of deposits into cash.

One of the complications here was that Bear Sterns, along with a handful of other organisations prominent in securities business, called itself 'an investment *bank*'.[10] In general, central banks should avoid making loans to investment banks. Central banks do not normally supervise or regulate these risky and aggressive organisations, while investment banks do not finance their assets by means of retail deposits. A serious difficulty for public policy arises if investment banks and commercial banks are owned by a 'bank holding company' or so-called 'universal bank'. The management of bank holding companies is complex, not least because their main boards have to allocate capital between the two types of 'banking'. If heavy losses are suffered in the securities trading and underwriting side of a universal bank, there is a temptation to transfer capital from the commercial bank in order

10   The word 'bank' is ambiguous. The phrase 'investment bank' is of US origin and had no currency in the City of London and the UK until the 1980s. The trading and underwriting of securities, which are the kernel of investment banking, were carried out in the UK by organisations with quite different names, i.e. 'jobbers' (for traders in securities) and 'merchant banks' (for underwriters of securities).

to shore up the securities operations. That undermines the extent to which depositors are protected by the bank's assets and so threatens financial stability.

But this is only one of the many conflicts of interest which seem to be endemic in universal banking. In the closing stage of the Great Depression the US Congress passed the Banking Act of 1933, sponsored by Senator Glass and Congressman Steagall, which mandated the separation of investment and commercial banking. The repeal of the 1933 Banking Act in 1999 has been followed by the formation of several large financial conglomerates, notably Citibank, which embrace investment banking, commercial banking and various other financial activities. The prominence of these conglomerates in the dot.com excesses of 2000 and 2001, and in the sub-prime crisis of 2007 and 2008, cannot be overlooked. While the subject is hugely controversial, any central bank must be wary of lending to a bank holding company. The money may be intended to protect depositors, but there is a danger that it will be swallowed by the more speculative activities of securities traders. Indeed, a case can be made that experience over the last decade confirms the wisdom of the Glass–Steagall arrangements and suggests that financial regulation should keep the two types of so-called 'banking' apart.[11] (Note that the separation of clearing business and retail deposit-taking from investment banking may not require primary legislation. The central bank may be able to enforce it by telling bank holding companies – and of course the counterparties from which they borrow – that their investment banking activities disqualify them

---

11   The remarks in this paragraph are controversial. For a very different view, see Charles Calomiris, *US Bank Deregulation in Historical Perspective*, Cambridge University Press, Cambridge and New York, 2000, especially chapters 4 and 5.

from last-resort lending in a crisis. Somehow this threat has to be credible in fair-weather conditions.)

The loan to AIG was even more extraordinary than that to J. P. Morgan to support the rescue of Bear Sterns. Again, it was necessary because of the linkages between the operations of the borrowing company on the one hand, and the solvency of the banking system and integrity of the payments mechanism on the other. Because AIG had guaranteed mortgage bonds held by banks and other financial institutions, AIG's survival was important to the valuation of these bonds, and hence to the value of many banks' and financial institutions' assets and capital. So, very unusually, the central bank may lend outside the deposit-taking banking system. The rationale is the same as last-resort lending to banks, to protect payments mechanisms and the convertibility of bank deposits into cash.

What are the right terms for lender-of-last-resort loans?

If it is agreed that in a crisis the most fitting recipients of lender-of-last-resort lending are deposit-taking banks and, in particular, clearing banks, on what terms should such lending be made? The key prescription synthesises two rules proposed by Bagehot in *Lombard Street*, which was a response to the 1866 Overend crisis. (The Overend crisis was the last major run on a British bank before that on Northern Rock in 2007.) This study has no quarrel with the gist of 'the Bagehot rule', but some aspects of its application need to be spelt out in detail to make them relevant to today's conditions.

Bagehot saw that the Bank of England, the bank with the monopoly of the legal-tender note issue, was different from other banks. Specifically, two crises in 1847 and 1857 demonstrated that, if the bank of issue tried to maximise profits by aggressive expansion of its balance sheet, the result would be overissuance of money and inflation. The inflation might threaten the pound's link with gold. As discussed in the rebuttal of Smith's *The Rationale of Central Banking* in Chapter 2, the larger message was that, instead of maximising profits, the bank of issue ought to pursue public policy goals.[12] In a crisis commercial banks' customers withdrew cash (Bank of England notes) from their deposits because they feared their banks might go bust. Bagehot argued that, assuming the commercial banks were in fact solvent, the best method for the Bank of England to restore confidence was twofold. First, the Bank should extend loans 'at a very high rate of interest' in order to prevent 'applicants … who do not require it'. Second, advances 'should be made on all good banking securities, and as largely as the public ask for them'. Indeed, 'If it is known that the Bank of England is freely advancing on what in ordinary times is reckoned to be a good security – on what is then commonly pledged and easily convertible – the alarm of the solvent merchants and bankers will be stayed.'[13] These two injunctions are usually condensed into one, that 'in a run the central bank should lend cash to a solvent but illiquid bank at a penalty rate to whatever extent is necessary, as long as the loan is secured by good collateral'. Five features of this rule merit separate discussion.

---

12   See above, pp. 36–7.
13   Bagehot, op. cit., pp. 147–9.

i The level of the penalty

Bagehot wrote, rather imprecisely, about the need for 'a very high rate of interest'. This is conventionally translated nowadays into a requirement for a 'penalty rate' – that is, a rate above the understood market rate (such as the central bank's repo rate or the inter-bank rate). The size of the penalty is a matter of debate. The general intention is reasonably clear, that the penalty should be high enough to discourage frequent use of the central bank's facilities, but not so high as to imperil the survival of a borrowing bank.[14] The Bank of England's practice in the recent crisis has been to charge 100 basis points or more above its own rate, but the Federal Reserve has in the past offered what were effectively lender-of-last-resort facilities at 50 basis points over the Federal funds rate. Chapter 3 showed that – with the very low ratios of cash and capital to assets that characterised banking in the opening years of the 21st century – banks sometimes had an average return on assets of no more than 50 to 100 basis points. No final conclusion is reached here, but an argument can be made that – given the very low margins found in some types of modern banking (including the mortgage business in which Northern Rock specialised) – a penalty of 100 basis points or more is too high.

ii The quality of the collateral for the loan

Bagehot's own phrasing on this aspect was nuanced. He said that no 'advances need be made on which [the central bank] would

---

14   According to George in November 1993, '… any support we provide will be on terms that are as penal as we can make them, without precipitating the collapse we are trying to avoid'. Op. cit., p. 65.

ultimately lose' and emphasised the need for 'good security'. But he inserted the interesting caveat: 'what in ordinary times is reckoned to be' good security. In August and September 2007 the Bank of England made a great fuss about the quality of the collateral required before banks could take advantage of its facilities. Its governor claimed that rules that were too easy-going on collateral would encourage banks to hold low-grade, risky paper. He injected the phrase 'moral hazard' into the public debate with the implication that bankers were more likely to be sloppy in credit appraisal if they thought they could dump any asset on the Bank of England. (This topic is also discussed in the narrative account of the Northern Rock affair in the next chapter. See pp. 122–4.)

Much depends on the type of central bank loan being made. In the event of a short-duration repo facility where the central bank's counterparty is an undoubtedly solvent bank, it surely matters little *to the behaviour of the commercial banks* what securities are offered. As the commercial bank is contractually bound to buy back the securities at an early date, the risk on the securities continues, for all intents and purposes, to lie with that bank. The issue of moral hazard then hardly arises. The same general argument applies whenever the central bank is lending to a solvent bank, since the central bank would normally be a preferred creditor. A central bank extends loans which must be repaid in full or purchases securities at market prices; it does not give grants to commercial banks. A loan is not a gift. So the potential availability of lender-of-last-resort facilities from the central bank does *not* reduce the incentives for the management of commercial banks to hold assets that will *ultimately* repay in full (i.e. with very low default probability).

But the general argument is subject to a serious qualification.

As Chapter 3 demonstrated, the potential availability of central bank facilities does affect commercial banks' management of their liquidity. A casual official attitude towards the collateral for central bank loans may be a mistake, but the nature of the mistake needs to be carefully stated. The problem is not that an easy-going stance by the central bank causes commercial banks to acquire assets with a high default probability, but rather that it tempts them to acquire assets that during their lives can be bought and sold only with difficulty and expense (i.e. that are illiquid). A distinction must be drawn between the default probability and liquidity characteristics of banks' assets.[15]

If a central bank relaxes its rules on collateral, commercial banks will raise the proportion of illiquid assets to total assets. Almost certainly, that will sooner or later lead to the central bank being asked to lend against securities, which – however low their default probability – have long residual lives, and are expensive to buy and sell. As the assessment of such securities' value may be complex and resource intensive (in terms of the professional time and so on needed to understand them), the central bank may – perhaps reasonably – be reluctant to accept them as collateral. But it is important to diagnose the situation correctly. The problem is not that the existence of a lender of last resort has undermined banks' incentives to acquire assets with low default probability. Rather it is that the central bank, which has its own capital at risk, does not have the resources to appraise all the

---

15 The academic theory of portfolio selection has tended to concentrate on the choice between risk and return, but in banking the liquidity characteristics of assets are fundamental. The subject of liquidity is neglected in modern finance theory. The point is made by the former treasurer of Barclays Bank, Brandon Davies, in 'Central bank liquidity provision as a public–private partnership', *Lombard Street Research Monthly Review*, 230, July 2008.

assets that the commercial banks want to offer as collateral. The difficult policy question relates to *the behaviour of the central bank*. In the years leading up to the 2007 crisis banks did indeed start to hold some weird and esoteric paper, and some of this paper was included in their accounts as 'available for sale' (i.e. as part of their liquidity).[16] As will emerge in the next chapter, this had important consequences in the Northern Rock affair and the wider crisis in the banking system.

It should be noted that, in all of this section, the discussion has been about repurchase operations or last-resort loans where repayment is expected. The matter is very different if the central bank has to purchase securities outright. If it is to make outright purchases of securities, it must of course be confident that the securities are of good quality and that the issuer will pay. But – by definition – an outright purchase of a security does not require the lodging of collateral by the seller, so the discussion of collateral is irrelevant. The matter is discussed further in Chapter 7.

iii The duration of the facility

Bagehot had little to say about how long a lender-of-last-resort loan should last. Since he was the pioneer of the lender-of-last-resort concept and had much else to say, the omission is excusable. Since the 1870s many countries, including the UK, have

---

16   In mid-2007 even large retail deposit-takers, such as the Royal Bank of Scotland and HBOS, had substantial holdings of so-called 'Alt-A' securities, backed by mortgage pools where the borrowers were known to have offered incomplete documentation. The securities were invariably triple-A and ought to pay back in full, but their very nature hardly inspired confidence. The problem is not new. In Chapter XII of *Lombard Street*, Bagehot noted that 'Mercantile bills are an exceedingly difficult kind of security to understand' (op. cit., p. 190).

suffered various permutations of banking system trauma. Interventions by the state – sometimes by the central bank, sometimes by the government, sometimes by the two acting in unison – have been common. The core objective has nearly always been financial stability, to maintain the convertibility of bank deposits into legal-tender notes. Experience has shown that the state's intervention may have to last many years.

Reference has already been made to the Bank of England's successful launching of the so-called 'lifeboat' in the secondary banking crisis of the mid-1970s; the final vestiges of that crisis were still being tidied up in the late 1980s. In late 1984 the Johnson Matthey Bank, an offshoot of the metal refining group Johnson Matthey, was insolvent and the Bank of England bought it for £1 in order to ensure that its affairs were run down in an orderly fashion; a small team of the Bank's officials oversaw Johnson Matthey for the next fifteen years. In the early 1990s a number of minor British banks, with their solvency threatened by a cyclical slide in property values, sought help from the Bank of England and in some cases received it; an article about the regulatory approach to these institutions appeared in the Bank's *Financial Stability Review* some years later in 1996, when the outcomes were still not certain in all cases.[17] So the norm in the UK, even in the last few decades, has been that the resolution of lender-of-last-resort episodes takes years, not months. The same lesson emerges clearly from the international record. In the 1990s the solvency of banking systems in both Japan and Sweden was undermined by real estate slumps, and possible bank runs had to be checked by government guarantees on their deposits. The

17   Patricia Jackson, 'Deposit protection and bank failures in the United Kingdom', *Financial Stability Review*, 1, Autumn 1996, Bank of England, London, pp. 38–43.

guarantees were in place for seven years in Japan and four years in Sweden.

The right principle for policymaking is surely simple. The extension of a lender-of-last-resort loan by the central bank to a private bank is virtually costless to society, but it has the merit of giving the private sector bank concerned time to reorganise its affairs and, all being well, to repay its depositors in full. As Sir John Hicks, the British economist who won the Nobel Prize in 1972, remarked in one of his later lectures, 'The social function of liquidity is that it gives time to think.'[18] The full repayment of depositors from the borrowing bank's own assets is what matters. It follows that lender-of-last-resort assistance must last as long as is necessary for the sensible and profitable resolution of the borrowing bank's affairs. Hurry and pressure are misplaced. In a speech in November 1993 at the London School of Economics, Sir Edward (now Lord) George said that the Bank of England wanted a visible and clearly defined exit for any loan to a troubled institution. But does it need to be pointed out that commercial banks are owned by shareholders and run by managements who have assets and livelihoods at stake? They approach a central bank for help only when things are awful, when – in other words – an exit is invisible and cannot be defined. The reality is that the Bank of England, like other central banks, has often become involved in bank rescues when it has little idea how long the rescue operation will last.

---

18   John Hicks, *The Crisis in Keynesian Economics*, Basil Blackwell, Oxford, 1974, p. 57.

iv The secrecy of the facility

The terms of most significant contracts between businesses are confidential, even when the businesses' reputations are not in jeopardy. When a commercial bank borrows from a central bank, its reputation is very much in jeopardy. Indeed, the publication of the mere existence of the loan may undermine the success of the transaction, since it symptomises balance-sheet weakness and may scare off other creditors. It was therefore logical that in his 1993 statement on the lender-of-last-resort function George said that last-resort loans should be secret, as far as possible. The difficulty is that the Bank of England has to publish its own balance sheet at regular intervals, for all sorts of good reasons. Secrecy may be possible for loans to small banks (as, for example, in the early 1990s), but it is almost certainly unsustainable for loans to large banks. A loan like that to Northern Rock, which peaked at almost £30 billion, would quickly be spotted. Goodhart has proposed that central banks publish data showing several categories of loan (different period to maturity, different forms of collateralisation), none of which would be particularly newsworthy.[19] This may be part of the answer. Almost certainly the central bank should not draw public attention to any last-resort facilities it extends, because of the danger of provoking a run. On the other hand, the concealment of a facility may favour one bank (say, the bank deemed to qualify for a last-resort loan) over another (a bank deemed not to qualify) and be anti-competitive. These matters are contentious and may always be so.

---

19 Goodhart's proposal appeared in a 2007 paper published by the London School of Economics, Financial Markets Group.

v The degree of contractual commitment

One of central bankers' favourite phrases is 'constructive ambiguity'. Its usual context is to let banks know that the Bank of England has discretion about whether a last-resort loan will be extended or not. The thinking is that the more uncertain the business environment in which banks are operating, the higher the quality of the assets they will choose to hold. To link two favourite catchphrases, the function of 'constructive ambiguity' is to limit the problem of 'moral hazard'.

But catchphrases come cheap. The next chapter will review the doctrine of constructive ambiguity very critically, while the supposed relevance of last-resort facilities to moral hazard in banks' asset selection has already been questioned. Interestingly, Bagehot was lukewarm about constructive ambiguity. Some of the sharpest rhetoric in *Lombard Street* was directed against the Bank of England's failure after the 1866 crisis to clarify how it would react to a similar event in future. One theme of *Lombard Street* was that, if a run on the banking system developed, the central bank could not behave like commercial banks and shrink assets. On the contrary, its job was to lend aggressively, expand its balance sheet and restore confidence. This was in fact how the Bank of England reacted to the 1866 crisis, with beneficial results all round. But the Bank did not then accept an explicit and permanent lender-of-last-resort role, causing Bagehot to rant against it in Chapter VIII of *Lombard Street*. In his words, 'it seems exceedingly strange that so important a responsibility should be unimposed, unacknowledged, and denied'.[20]

---

20   Bagehot, op. cit., p.. 129.

In summary ...

To summarise, last-resort loans – loans in cash to solvent but illiquid banks – should be

1. at a rate high enough to discourage frequent use of such facilities, but not so high as needlessly to undermine the solvency of the troubled institutions;
2. secured on collateral that is good 'in normal times', even if it has a jaundiced reputation in the crisis period;
3. extended for as long as necessary for the orderly and profitable resolution of the borrowing banks' affairs, with the priority being to maximise the value of the banks' assets and not to accelerate the loans' repayment;
4. confidential, as far as possible; and
5. subject to a clear contractual framework with as little uncertainty as possible.

One final observation is needed. The Bank of England evolved as a central bank because bankers had a need for a certain type of banking service. In this sense the Bank of England is a commercial organisation which has customers, despite being owned by the state and having public policy objectives. For all the ambivalence of its position as both part of the British constitution and a business with a balance sheet, its relationship with the banking industry ought to be friendly and cooperative. If the Bank behaves towards the commercial banks in too heavy-handed a fashion, they have the option to deploy their capital in other countries or to switch it to other profit-making opportunities in the UK.

What about bust banks?

This chapter has proceeded so far on the assumption that last-resort lending is to solvent institutions and so is highly certain of being repaid in due course. But what if the bank asking for a last-resort loan is or may be bust?

The tense is important here. It matters hugely whether the bank 'is' or 'may be' bust. If a bank is bust, a last-resort loan to it may not be repaid in full. The central bank may therefore incur a loss on the loan and a reduction in capital. The central bank may deem this acceptable, if the result is that the public's confidence in bank deposits is reinforced and the reputation of the whole system enhanced. (As noted above, this was the justification for the Bank of England's loss-making rescue of Williams Deacon's in the early 1930s.) But far worse outcomes can be imagined. If many banks are bust, the extension of numerous last-resort loans may result in the elimination of the central bank's capital. In a situation of widespread and comprehensive insolvency, the resolution of various creditors' interests is almost certain to involve appeal to the courts and perhaps to the legislature. All financial relationships become litigious and politicised. The usual guidelines for resource allocation are likely to break down, causing immense damage to economic efficiency.

The Great Depression in the USA between 1929 and 1933 led to the closure of thousands of banks and their failure to repay depositors in full. The Federal Deposit Insurance Corporation (FDIC) was established in 1934, in order to create a fund that could in future compensate depositors for losses of this kind. The fund was financed in the first instance by a loan of $3 billion from the US Treasury, but over time by annual levies (equal to a low percentage of total deposits) on banks. (Three billion dollars may sound like a small sum, but in 1933 the USA's GNP was under $60 billion, so the FDIC's initial resources from the state were about 5 per cent of GNP.) Over the next 45 years the level of bank failures declined dramatically in the USA. Deposit insurance was almost universally regarded as a success and as having made an essential contribution to American prosperity in the early post-war decades. Some economists have been tempted by this record to regard deposit insurance as not merely vital to financial stability, but as a full-scale substitute for central banking. This notion – that a well-funded deposit insurance agency is an alternative to a central bank – will be discussed in more detail in the next chapter.[21] For the moment a dichotomy may be proposed, that the central bank's function is to extend last-resort loans to solvent but illiquid banks whereas the deposit insurance agency's task is to compensate depositors for shortfalls in the value of their deposits at insolvent banks.

But what about banks that 'may be' bust? In the earlier discussion it was argued that on the whole last-resort loans cannot be expected to have a 'visible exit'. Almost by definition a facility is a last-resort loan when, on normal market terms, the exit is invisible. Many volumes have been written about how last-resort episodes have been, can be and should be resolved. Suffice it to say that the lack of visibility in these episodes has two main aspects: uncertainty about the value of a bank's assets and uncertainty about the length of time needed to maximise that value. When a central bank lends to a troubled commercial bank, it sometimes happens that the troubled bank has a deficiency of equity and,

---

21 As mentioned in note 12 to Chapter 1, the classic academic paper in defence of deposit insurance is that published by Diamond and Dybvig in *Journal of Political Economy* in 1983.

strictly speaking, is 'bust' in accounting and legal terms. Recovery may, however, still be a reasonable prospect.

The value of the bank's assets may at present be so far beneath that of the deposit liabilities that shareholder funds have been wiped out. But the value of the bank's assets depends partly on the value of the collateral behind its loans and that in turn depends on larger macroeconomic forces. Typically banks lend against security that has a value higher – say, 30, 50 or even 100 per cent more – than the loan principal. If mortgage banks' loan-to-value ratio (that is, the ratio of the loan principal relative to the value of the security, such as a house in mortgage borrowing) starts at 75 per cent, they can tolerate a 25 per cent drop in house prices before they risk losses on their loan portfolios. But, even if house prices go down by 40 per cent, that is not the end of the story. Most mortgage borrowers are reluctant to leave their homes, because of the emotional upheaval and transactions costs involved. House prices may fall by 40 per cent between 2007 and 2010, and rise by two-thirds between 2010 and 2015. They are back to their 2007 level by 2015. Banks' security would therefore be restored to the original position, even if homeowners had repaid none of the mortgage principal. In practice homeowners are likely to have repaid a significant proportion of their mortgages and banks' security on the 2007-vintage loans is still good after eight years of housing-market turmoil. The larger point is that banks' solvency depends on asset values. A bank that appears to be bust given the general level of asset prices in 2009 may have eliminated its loan losses when assets are valued at 2015 prices.

Further, it must be remembered that banks' losses from bad loans are – in the normal course of events – offset by operating profits. As discussed in Chapter 3, the operating profits arise from the excess of the interest received on the loan portfolio, plus an assortment of fees, over costs that consist of interest paid on deposits and operating expenses (staff costs, rent and so on). It is not unusual for operating profits to run at 1.5 per cent of assets. As a result, with a loan write-off rate of 0.5 per cent of assets and a 5 per cent capital/assets ratio, the rate of return on capital is 20 per cent (1.5 minus 0.5, divided by 5 and multiplied by 100). Suppose that a hit of some sort – say a sudden drop in the value of a bank's securities equal to 3 per cent of assets – reduces its capital to 2 per cent of assets. Superficially, the bank is in a bad way, not least because a 2 per cent capital/assets ratio is well below conventional regulatory minima. Regulators may intervene and require the bank to cut its stock of lending. (They would almost certainly be misguided in doing so, but that may not stop them.)

As long as the operating profit persists at 1.5 per cent of assets, it is obvious that the bank can not only survive a hit amounting to 60 per cent of its capital, but can do so quite quickly without shedding any assets. The bank must be discouraged by its regulators from making any dividend payment. With all its operating profit retained, its capital/assets ratio is back to 5 per cent after a mere three years. Life can then go on as before. Of course, at the start of the process, when the bank has lost 60 per cent of its capital (and in all probability its share price has dived), the successful outcome may be impossible to see. The desired ultimate 'exit' may be invisible. But – clearly and indisputably – a last-resort loan would have been justified if the afflicted bank could not otherwise have funded its assets. In the case under discussion that loan would have been needed for only three years, but in many other cases the facilities may have to last several years until depositors' confidence is restored. So the eventual length of the last-resort loan, the period that turns out to be necessary for the return to conventional patterns of funding, depends not only on such macroeconomic variables as movements in house prices and the stock market, but also on the level of banks' ongoing operating profits relative to their loan losses.

The message seems to be that last-resort lending is complex and resists glib generalisations. While some broad principles can be stated, each case is individual and must be assessed on its own merits. This section now ends with a proposition that may seem paradoxical. Chapter 3 showed that until the middle years of the current decade banks had economised on both cash and capital to a degree that would have astonished early bankers. Banks with a cash ratio of under 1 per cent and a capital/asset ratio of 5 per cent appear extraordinarily fragile. If they lose only £1 out of every £20 in their assets, they are ostensibly 'bust'. But the last few paragraphs have argued that – if asset values are on a long-run upward trend (and asset values are on such a trend in most dynamic capitalist societies), and if they can consistently achieve operating profits of more than, say, 1 per cent of assets – banks are also resilient. They can take quite big hits to their capital and yet bounce back. In banking, time is a great healer. It follows that the central bank may sometimes be correct to extend a last-resort loan to a bank that, in strict accounting terms, is bust. In Goodhart's words, '... on a number of occasions financial institutions have been effectively insolvent, but so long as everyone steadfastly averted their gaze, a way through and back to solvency was achieved'.[22] Much depends on analysis of balance sheets, default probabilities and the like, but judgement – judgement based on

---

22 Goodhart, 'Why do banks need a central bank?', *Oxford Economic Papers*, 39, 1987, p. 87.

decades of banking experience – is also valuable. The conclusion cannot be escaped. The lender-of-last-resort function needs to be performed, to a large extent, by people who have worked in banks for many years and have been through cyclical vicissitudes a few times. The senior staff of a central bank should include a decent proportion of bankers.

What about the nationalisation of troubled banks?

When the Northern Rock crisis broke in September 2007 some newspaper commentators advocated immediate nationalisation, even though Northern Rock was undoubtedly solvent in the sense of having an excess of assets over non-equity liabilities. These commentators – who included Martin Wolf of the *Financial Times* and Anatole Kaletsky of *The Times* – appeared to be vindicated on 18 February 2008, when nationalisation was announced. Nationalisation brought to an end the sorry saga of abortive takeover negotiations and partisan political point-scoring which is narrated in more detail in the next chapter. When in September 2008 a similar crisis seemed liable to erupt over Bradford & Bingley, the Tripartite Authorities were more decisive. Although Bradford & Bingley had just received the proceeds of a large rights issue and 97 per cent of its loans were current (i.e. not in arrears), it was nationalised without further ado.

Even more dramatic were the events of October 2008. All of Britain's large banks were told by regulators to increase their capital, in anticipation of a possible severe recession. If they were unable to raise the money from private sources, officialdom required them to issue securities on unfavourable terms, and to sell some or all of these securities to the government. Robert Peston, the BBC journalist whose stories had provoked the run on Northern Rock, put out stories about the nationalisation, or part-nationalisation, of the British banking system. These stories, like the damaging Northern Rock leak, were usually published in advance of any official press release on the government's actions and tended to be misleading. (Wolf, Kaletsky and Peston failed to distinguish in their journalism between banks' 'liquidity' and 'solvency', and hence to explain to their audience the crucial difference between an insolvent and an illiquid bank. They were not alone in this omission. An annex below is intended to clarify the subject.)

The nationalisation of solvent banks is a bad idea, for at least four reasons. First, the vulnerability of such banks to political pressures of various kinds undermines their ability to choose assets on commercial criteria and so to improve the allocation of resources. A constant refrain over many years in World Bank and IMF research publications, and in more specialist monographs in development finance, is that the efficiency of resource use is undermined by state ownership of banks.[23] Second, the globalisation of finance has made international regulators anxious to preserve fair competition between the banks of different nations. But state-owned banks have the improper advantage that their largest shareholder cannot go bust and, hence, have to be made subject to various bureaucratic restrictions on their operation.[24]

Third, if nationalisation takes place without shareholders'

---

23 The author discussed the effects of state ownership of the banking systems of several Latin American economies in ch. 2 of his 1985 study, *Economic Liberalism in the Cone of Latin America*, Trade Policy Research Centre, London.

24 After it had come into state ownership, Northern Rock's operations were subject to a code governing the operations of state-owned banks formulated by the European Commission in Brussels. Again, the author discussed this in his 2008 pamphlet *Northern Rock and the European Union*, op. cit., pp. 12–14.

consent, difficult issues are raised about the appropriate procedure for compensation. With both Northern Rock and Bradford & Bingley, shareholder consent was not obtained. Moreover, it was explicitly threatened in the October 2008 recapitalisation exercise that, again, the government would nationalise the banks without shareholders' consent if they resisted its pressure. Northern Rock, Bradford & Bingley and the big banks caught up in the hubbub of October 2008 were solvent and profitable at the time they were nationalised or threatened with nationalisation. Shareholders and management felt angry that they were forced by the government to dilute their property rights. Finally, and as a consequence of the third point, the apparent insecurity of property rights in the UK's financial sector will persuade banks to relocate internationally mobile business to other nations. The result will be declines in output and employment in the UK banking industry, and in the tax revenues that it pays to the British government.

The correct principles of public policy in this area are twofold. First, the best way to help solvent but illiquid banks is for the central bank to extend last-resort loans in accordance with the Bagehot principles. Because such loans are at penalty rates, borrowers are motivated to repay as soon as possible. An important merit of last-resort loans is that they neither challenge shareholders' rights nor undermine the maximisation incentives of a market economy. Their administrative and political sequel is therefore likely to be far less problematic than that which follows nationalisation. Second, nationalisation should occur only when a bank is irredeemably insolvent. The last section showed that banks are surprisingly resilient in the medium term (i.e. over a period of several years) however badly they are hit (say, in a particular year) by asset write-offs, because their net interest income – the main component of operating profits – has some resemblance to an annuity. (Banks' debtors must service the loans or otherwise lose the collateral they have offered.) Since Northern Rock and Bradford & Bingley were not irredeemably insolvent when nationalised, the eventual resolution of these banks' affairs is likely to involve further tension between banks' shareholders and the British state. This tension is now only one aspect of a larger hostility between bankers and politicians, which will undermine UK banks' efficiency and international competitiveness. A provisional verdict on the official interventions in UK banking in 2007 and 2008 is that, when governments nationalise in haste, they are likely to repent at leisure.[25]

Annex: the distinction between insolvency and illiquidity in banking

Discussion of the banking crisis of 2007 and 2008 was handicapped by the misuse of words. The word 'solvency' has a different significance in banking from that in everyday parlance. According to a recent edition of *The Penguin Concise English Dictionary*, the meaning of 'solvency' is 'ability to pay all debts'. On this basis Northern Rock appeared in September 2007 to be insolvent, since it was having trouble paying depositors back with cash. In that sense, it was not *immediately* 'able to pay all debts'. In the banking industry, however, the term 'solvency' has a specific connotation

---

25 In the author's opinion (in November 2008) the British government is likely to make large capital gains on the shareholdings in British banks that it acquired in late 2008. But the damage to the efficiency and competitiveness of the UK banking industry is already serious and will increase. A redistribution of wealth from bank shareholders to the rest of the population is under way, but in the long run the nation as a whole will be the loser.

which needs to be elaborated with care. Indeed, the practice in banking is to assess financial soundness by two separate tests, 'solvency' and 'liquidity'.

Commercial banks – like every other business organisation – must

- *either* have assets that belong to their shareholders (i.e. equity) and no one else
- *or* expect within a reasonably short period of normal trading to have built up positive equity belonging to shareholders,

if they are to trade without misleading creditors. The relevant entry in the balance sheet is of 'capital' (or 'capital and reserves' or a cognate term) on the liabilities side of the balance sheet. As discussed earlier in Chapter 3, nowadays banks' equity capital is commonly less than 5 per cent of their assets.

A bank is said to be 'solvent' if the value of its assets exceeds the value of its liabilities other than those to equity shareholders. Further, the concept of 'solvency' is measured by the capital (and more specifically by the equity capital) item on the liabilities side of the balance sheet. A bank is insolvent if it has no equity capital (or no reasonable prospect of having positive equity capital in the foreseeable future) and so cannot repay all depositors at par *because of an insufficiency of assets*.

The term 'liquidity' has a multiplicity of meanings, but for brevity it can be understood to relate particularly to the cash item on the assets side of the balance sheet. If some cash is there (either in the vaults or in the cash reserve at the central bank), the bank can repay at least some depositors with cash. A bank is illiquid if it has no cash in its vaults or in its central bank reserve and so

Figure 4 **Insolvency and illiquidity in banking**
£ million

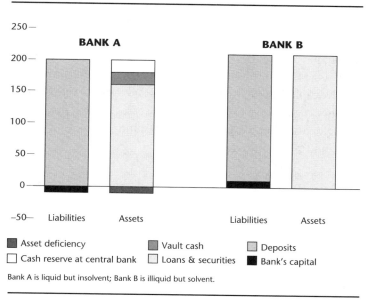

Bank A is liquid but insolvent; Bank B is illiquid but solvent.

cannot repay all depositors at par *because of an insufficient cash holding.*

It is evident that 'solvency' and 'liquidity' are different ideas. Journalists and even distinguished commentators sometimes have trouble with the distinction, despite its fundamental character. (An example of the muddle was an observation in a story in the *Sunday Times* of 21 September 2008, on 'Short sellers clear despite ban' by James Ashton, that the FSA was 'consulting on changes to capital ratios – the amount of cash banks hold in reserve'.) A bank can be 'insolvent' (i.e. with negative capital) but 'liquid' (i.e. with a high ratio of cash to assets), and 'illiquid' (i.e. without any cash in its tills) but 'solvent' (i.e. with positive capital), as is illustrated in Figure 4. This unfortunately makes the interpretation of banks' financial viability difficult and confusing compared with that of most commercial organisations. In particular, there is a temptation to describe organisations that have difficulty financing their assets as 'insolvent' or 'bust', when they not only have positive capital, but have positive capital sufficient to comply with solvency regulations. (There are also degrees of both insolvency and illiquidity, but discussion of the resulting nuances of definition could take many pages.)

6 THE NORTHERN ROCK CRISIS

As explained in Chapter 1, the Northern Rock crisis was followed by proposals to change the structure of banking regulation, and at the time of writing this was being translated into actual legislation in the 2008 Banking Reform Act. This study is a contribution to the debate about the upheaval in British banking. But a further account of the antecedents to the crisis, and indeed of the crisis itself, is needed to set the debate properly in context.

UK banks' liquidity in the lightly regulated environment from the mid-1990s

Chapter 3 documented the huge declines in UK banks' cash-to-asset ratios in the second half of the twentieth century; it also noted that from the mid-1990s there was little official concern about how banks organised their second line of defence, the ratio of liquid assets to total assets. Towards the end of the period, liquidity management was made more difficult by untoward developments in the availability of asset types, in which the banks had little say. In the nineteenth century and for nearly all of the twentieth century two types of asset had been staples in the organisation of banks' balance sheets: short-dated claims on the government, especially Treasury bills, and so-called 'eligible bills'.[1] Both assets were very low-risk and, as remarked in Chapter 3, could be readily sold to the Bank of England for cash. As they were certain to trade close to their par value and cost next to nothing to buy or sell, they epitomised the concept of 'liquidity'.

Treasury bills and short-dated government securities ('gilts') were free from default risk simply because they were claims on government, and the relatively short period to redemption limited the susceptibility of their price to yield changes; eligible bills were issued by private sector companies, but their usual initial period to redemption was only three months and their default risk was 'accepted' by two high-quality banking names.[2] (This is the origin of both the term 'accepting houses' and the name of the Anthony Powell novel *The Acceptance World*.[3]) By the middle of the twentieth century the Bank of England had hardly any staff able to assess credit risk, but in transactions in Treasury bills, gilts and eligible bills that did not matter. In addition, a special type of institution – the discount houses – existed as a buffer between the commercial banks and the Bank of England. The discount houses' assets were almost entirely Treasury bills, short-dated gilts and commercial bills, while their liabilities were mostly deposits from banks,

1   Eligible bills were a kind of commercial bill. They were called 'eligible' because they were eligible for sale to (or 'rediscount at') the Bank of England.

2   The Bank of England used to publish a list of banks that could 'accept' commercial bills and so make them eligible for rediscount. A similar system was established in the USA, where two-name bankers' acceptances could be rediscounted at the Federal Reserve. As far as the author is aware, the two-name feature of this paper has meant that it has never defaulted either in the USA or the UK, but he may be wrong.

3   'The Acceptance World was the world in which the essential element – happiness, for example – is drawn, as it were, from an engagement to meet a bill.' Anthony Powell, *The Acceptance World*, Fontana, London, 1983 (originally published in 1955), p. 178.

known as 'money-at-call'.[4] As a result of these arrangements, British banks' liquidity consisted of three assets: appropriate government securities (i.e. Treasury bills and short-dated gilts), eligible bills and money-at-call with the discount houses.

In the closing decades of the twentieth century and opening years of the 21st century the ratio of public debt to national income fell sharply, while insurance companies and pension funds asked the government (or from 1998 its Debt Management Office) to bias new issuance towards the long end. The availability of Treasury bills and short-dated gilts to the banking system declined markedly compared with the situation mid-century. Commercial bills continued to be issued in abundance in the 1980s, but in the 1990s the Treasury and the Bank of England decided to bring the discount market to an end.[5] The discount houses wound down their very liquid assets and their money-at-call liabilities, and transferred their capital to other activities. In 1997 the London Money Market Association, dominated by banks as such, replaced the London Discount Market Association. Further, in 2003 the Bank of England brought the apparatus of bill eligibility to a close, apparently on the grounds that entries for bills in its accounts were now very small and clogged up computer

4   Perhaps the discount market's most important social benefits were, first, that a new bank could easily enter British banking by leaving money-at-call with a discount house, and, second, that the Bank of England could 'inject liquidity into the system' (i.e. credit sums to the discount houses' balances with it), without selecting any particular lending bank as the destination of the funds (in principle discount houses bought bills, but did not themselves initiate loans). Both features were pro-competitive. The point was noted by Goodhart in 'Myths about the lender of last resort role', *International Finance*, 2(3), Blackwell, Oxford, 1999, reprinted as pp. 227–45 in Charles Goodhart and Gerhard Illing, *Financial Crises, Contagion, and the Lender of Last Resort*, Oxford University Press, Oxford, 2002. See, particularly, p. 230.

5   No formal announcement was made.

systems. So by the middle years of the current decade the three traditional forms of UK bank liquidity had largely disappeared.

But one lesson from Chapter 3 cannot be evaded. While commercial banks always need cash to meet deposit withdrawals and for inter-bank settlement, they try to maintain holdings of liquid assets which earn some income as well as being easily convertible into cash. The opening years of the 21st century saw a boom in so-called 'structured finance', in which banking groups bought up baskets of mortgages, hire purchase assets and other streams of receivable cash, and issued debt liabilities against them.[6] The debt liabilities – the ABS, the CDOs and the CMOs mentioned in Chapter 1 – were cut up into tranches of different 'seniority'. The most senior debt tranche would have the first claim on the assets if there were any defaults, a second tranche would have the second claim and a junior (or so-called 'equity') tranche would pick up the residual assets. Given that most people service home mortgages through thick and thin, the most senior debt ought to have been – and usually was – awarded a triple-A rating by the credit rating agencies. A triple-A rating ought to put such paper on the same pedestal, in terms of credit standing, as government securities. In view of the dearth of Treasury bills, the

6   As mentioned in note 2 above, in the traditional system of UK bank liquidity management paper issued by the private sector – i.e. two-name eligible paper – could be and was used extensively in Bank of England open-market operations. The two-name feature was a do-it-yourself form of credit endorsement without any conflicts of interest. (The acceptor took a fee, but was at risk until the bill was repaid.) By contrast, the creditworthiness of the triple-A securities bought by banks in the structured finance boom was judged by credit rating agencies, although these agencies suffered from a severe conflict of interests. (The company to be rated paid the fee.) The case for the revival of bill eligibility was made by the author and Brandon Davies, a former treasurer of Barclays Bank, in 'How to restore liquidity to triple-A securities', *Financial Times*, 17 September 2008.

complete absence of eligible bills and the demise of the discount market, how were UK banks to satisfy their need for liquid assets? It is understandable, even if it turned out to be disastrous, that over the last decade or so they have decided to hold large quantities of the triple-A securities created in the structured finance boom. Such securities were presented in banks' accounts as 'available for sale' and were seen as a substitute for traditional liquid assets.

Were the banks irresponsible in their behaviour? Chapter 3 showed that by the middle of the current decade UK banks had negligible cash holdings and, at least superficially, a perilous degree of maturity transformation in their balance sheets. In their defence banks' managements would have emphasised that they kept deposits at other banks plus the cushion of available-for-sale securities. Inter-bank deposits and available-for-sale securities could be viewed as similar in quality to the money-at-call and bill assets that would have qualified as 'liquid' in the eyes of the Bank of England in the mid-twentieth century. In fact, at the end of June 2007 even the much-criticised Northern Rock had deposits with other banks of £6,812 million and available-for-sale securities of £8,000 million, against a balance sheet total of £113,506 million.[7] So its 'liquid assets', taken altogether, were more than 13 per cent of liabilities (and much more than 13 per cent of retail deposits), not out of line with the norms of the late twentieth century. Furthermore, banks' executives might have noted that they had unused inter-bank 'lines' (i.e. borrowing facilities), which could be drawn if – for any reason – they could not find buyers for their supposedly 'available-for-sale' securities.

One flaw in these arrangements was that, while any individual

---

7   Northern Rock interim results, published on 25 July 2007 and available on the Northern Rock website, p. 19.

bank could regard an inter-bank line from other banks as enabling it quickly to add to its cash, for all banks together the inter-bank lines cancelled out. If all banks either ceased to trust each other or found that they needed cash for their own businesses, the likelihood was that they would cut their lines to each other. Inter-bank finance would prove illusory as a source of liquidity. Further, if the market in allegedly 'available-for-sale' securities became constipated by excess supply (of, for example, the ABS, CDOs and CMOs which were issued in vast quantities in 2005 and 2006) or were disrupted for some other reason, the only remaining liquid asset would be cash. That ultimate source of cash was the central bank, which in the UK context meant the Bank of England. The Bank of England's attitude towards the various forms of asset-backed paper would therefore be fundamental to banks' own management strategies and decisions.

The Bank of England breaks Bagehot's rule

After the international wholesale banking markets became paralysed on 9 August 2007, a number of British banks approached the Bank of England for an easing of its collateral requirements in repurchase operations. They received a dusty answer. For many years they had run down their cash holdings, taking it for granted that the Bank of England would always help them out as long as they had adequate capital and good-quality assets. This assumption was shattered by the insistence of Mervyn King, the Bank's governor, that only government securities constituted the right kind of collateral for central bank loans.[8] King's insistence was the

---

8   Alex Brummer, *The Crunch*, Random House, London, 2008, p. 66.

more remarkable in that it had been officialdom's failure to issue short-dated gilts in the previous five years which had been at least partly responsible for the banks' purchases of triple-A mortgage-backed paper. The banks realised that the assets that they deemed available-for-sale, and so as serving the same function as official 'liquid assets' in the past, would not find a willing buyer in the Bank of England.

In *Lombard Street*, Bagehot argued that in emergencies the Bank of England should 'lend ... as fast as' it can, because 'ready lending ... cures panics, and non-lending or niggardly lending ... aggravates them'.[9] King's action undoubtedly contravened the spirit of Bagehot's principles. Moreover, the Bank of England's behaviour was at variance with that of the world's two largest central banks, the Federal Reserve and the European Central Bank. Whereas the Bank of England insisted on government securities as loan collateral and charged 100 basis points above base rate for above-normal use of its borrowing facilities, the Fed and the ECB took a wide range of assets as collateral and deliberately injected large amounts into the money markets (i.e. they credited sums to banks' balances with them). King's approach has subsequently come in for heavy criticism. According to Alex Brummer in his book *The Crunch*, 'when it came to the practical side of banking – the provision of liquidity designed to prevent contagion – King was strangely out of touch'.[10]

Within a few weeks the Bank of England had relented on its collateral rules and adopted a position similar to that of the

---

9   Walter Bagehot, *Lombard Street*, vol.. IX in Norman St John-Stevas (ed.), *The Collected Works of Walter Bagehot*, The Economist, London, 1978 (originally published in 1873), p. 207.

10   Brummer, op. cit., p. 120.

two larger central banks. However, the damage had been done. British banks realised that their triple-A securities were not as high-quality as their traditional liquid assets. Inter-bank lines were being trimmed all through the spring and early summer of 2007, but the process was now intensified. Further, some banks sold off their triple-A securities in order to take in cash from other banks. These securities therefore fell to beneath their fair value, leading to losses for the banks. Under mark-to-market accounting rules, the banks were required to lower the value of their capital accordingly. This may sound like a technicality, but – for banks operating with a capital-to-assets ratio of 5 per cent – a loss on available-for-sale securities equal to only 1 per cent of assets wiped out 20 per cent of capital. If banks then responded to the cut in capital by restricting new lending, the growth of both bank credit and the quantity of money (which consists of banks' deposits) would suffer. Finally, the banks continued to believe that the great majority of the triple-A securities they held would pay back in full (100 cents in the dollar, 100 pence in the pound, and so on) at redemption. Since the securities were trading at prices well below fair value, the banks still holding triple-A securities decided to cling to them. Instead of being easy to buy and sell, like the Treasury bills, short-dated gilts and eligible bills that had been so prominent in banks' cash management twenty years earlier, in late 2007 many triple-A securities were not being bought or sold at all. With the market image of structured finance products blighted in this way, new issues of such products could no longer be made.

Northern Rock's predicament

For one British bank in particular, the harsher conditions in the inter-bank market and the cessation of structured finance issuance were disastrous. As noted in Chapter 1, the management of this bank – Northern Rock – was in an acute predicament. Because a securitisation issue planned for September could not now go ahead, Northern Rock might be unable to fund its assets. The details of the actions taken in August and September 2007 by the FSA – and indeed by its two partners in the Tripartite Authorities, the Bank of England and the Treasury – are to some degree confidential and may remain so for many years. A good narrative account based on personal interviews has, however, appeared in Alex Brummer's *The Crunch*.

The heart of Northern Rock's problem was that it lacked retail deposits on a sufficient scale from a large branch network: that was why the sudden halt in wholesale funding was so damaging. At the suggestion of Northern Rock's board, the FSA agreed that the American investment bank Merrill Lynch should seek a possible buyer. Merrill Lynch put a senior corporate finance executive, Matthew Greenberg, in charge of the job. He saw that an obvious candidate was Lloyds TSB, since it had both an extensive branch network and only slight involvement in the excesses of structured finance. According to Brummer, by early September Lloyds TSB was ready to go ahead with a bid of £2 a share. But Lloyds TSB's top management had an important reservation. Although their own bank did have a large branch network and was well capitalised, they were concerned that they might have difficulty funding Northern Rock's assets, particularly in 2009. They therefore asked for a Bank of England back-up loan facility of £30 billion, to be provided on commercial terms. These terms were presumably inter-bank or base rate plus a margin, but the details are not in the public domain. It must be emphasised that the facility – like the overdrafts discussed in Chapter 4 – might not have been used at all. Indeed, if the deal had gone ahead, Lloyds TSB would almost certainly have preferred not to draw on it, but to rely instead on retail deposits or other conventional types of funding.

A fair surmise is that – if Lloyds TSB had acquired Northern Rock – the run would not have happened and the Northern Rock fiasco might have been averted. To quote Brummer again, 'The Rock received the distinct impression from its regulator the FSA, its first point of contact [in officialdom], that this was a deal that could be done.'[11] The obstacle was the Bank of England. King was anxious that Lloyds TSB was being unduly favoured by the Tripartite Authorities and that European competition law was being broken. On Monday, 10 September 2007, Northern Rock and Lloyds TSB had almost completed the wording of a press release on a deal. But the next day the Bank of England's deputy governor, Sir John Gieve, phoned Northern Rock's chief executive and said that the £30 billion stand-by facility could not be granted. The deal was stymied. As Northern Rock had been expecting the deal to go ahead, its cash problem became urgent. By Thursday, 13 September, its executives agreed they would have to borrow from the Bank of England, and told FSA and Bank officials that a stock exchange announcement had to be made about a development so fundamental to its business. The announcement was due early on Friday, 14 September. Unfortunately, the Peston leak on the BBC both preceded it and gave a misleading impression of the gravity of Northern Rock's situation. The run followed in short order.

---

11   Ibid., p. 77.

Some fundamentals of central banking

In early 2007 Northern Rock had been a solvent, profitable and well-regulated bank. The closure of the wholesale money markets in August was a genuine shock which no one had foreseen with any clarity. According to the Bagehot rule, Northern Rock was an appropriate beneficiary of a lender-of-last-resort loan. It did indeed receive such a loan, eventually to top out at nearly £30 billion, in the weeks following 14 September. But the loan was granted virtually under duress, since without it Northern Rock's depositors could not have been repaid with legal-tender banknotes. There is no doubt that the outcome was unintended and embarrassing for officialdom.

In evidence to the Treasury Committee of the House of Commons on 20 September King said that the Bank of England would have liked to act as lender of last resort to Northern Rock in the same way that it had done in the so-called 'small banks crisis' of the early 1990s. In other words, the Bank would have liked the facility to be made covertly in order to minimise the risk of a run. He then referred to four pieces of legislation, two of them arising from the UK's membership of the European Union, as constraining the Bank's freedom to act. (A European Commissioner immediately disputed King's interpretation.[12]) But in fact, as the next few paragraphs will show, King disliked the whole idea of the Bank of England lending to shareholder-owned, profit-seeking banks.

The trouble started at King's mid-August meeting with the banks, where he turned down their request for an easing of collateral rules in repo transactions. That caused tension between the

---

12   Tim Congdon, *Northern Rock and the European Union*, Global Vision, London, 2008, p. 8.

Bank of England and the banks, and made them more reluctant to operate on the easy-going, give-and-take basis that had marked their relationship over the decades. In the secondary banking crisis of the mid-1970s the Bank of England persuaded the big clearing banks, with their retail funds, to lend to the secondary banks for a few years in the 'lifeboat' rescue.[13] As a result, the secondary banks were able to unwind their loan portfolios in a gradual and orderly way. The problems were largely hidden from public view, losses inside the banking industry were containable and banks' customers were able to convert deposits into notes at all times. The lifeboat operation, largely organised by the then governor, Sir Gordon (now Lord) Richardson, and the deputy governor, Sir Jasper Hollom, is widely regarded as a model of skilful central banking.

But – because of the animosity that arose from the mid-August meeting – it would have been impossible for King to have entered negotiations with the big banks in the same spirit as Richardson and Hollom over thirty years earlier.[14] Even worse was the Bank's interference, at a late and crucial stage, in the discussions between the FSA, Lloyds TSB and Northern Rock. At the senior level, banking supervision in the FSA was largely staffed by former Bank of England officials, many with considerable banking expertise. The FSA was correct to try to arrange a takeover of Northern Rock by a bank with undoubted strength in retail funding. The

---

13   The secondary banking crisis was also referred to in Chapter 5. See p. 91 above.

14   It is sometimes claimed that the club-like nature of British banking has been ended by the globalisation of finance, so that a lifeboat-type operation could not now be launched. But see p. 124 of Brummer's *The Crunch* for an account of a Sunday afternoon gathering of bankers in 1998, called by Eddie George (the then governor of the Bank of England), to handle the funding problems of Korean banks.

Bank of England loan facility requested by Lloyds TSB may or may not have been used, but it would not have attracted all the media hullabaloo of the loan to Northern Rock. Competition issues were relevant, but, if the Lloyds TSB takeover had been announced, there would have been many weeks for another bidder to emerge and the same Bank of England facility could have been made available to it.[15] Indeed, given officialdom's concern over competition issues in the mooted Lloyds TSB takeover of Northern Rock, it is staggering that such issues were brushed to one side in the much more anti-competitive Lloyds TSB takeover of HBOS in late 2008. The contrast between the state's attitude towards the two deals speaks volumes about the inconsistency verging on chaos in policymaking in this period.

In a speech to the Northern Ireland Chamber of Commerce in October 2007, King argued that Northern Rock had been at fault in not organising sufficient 'liquidity insurance'. What he meant by this was that it had not arranged large enough lines of unused inter-bank credit from big banks to anticipate a cash problem. He compared Northern Rock unfavourably with an American counterpart, Countrywide, which – in his words – on '17 August was able to claim on that insurance and draw down $11.5 billion of committed credit lines'. He alleged that Northern Rock had not taken out 'anything like that level of liquidity insurance'.[16] In its evidence to the Treasury Committee three weeks later Northern Rock refuted King point by point, emphasising that – relative to

---

15 According to Brummer, the decision not to offer a facility to Lloyds TSB was taken by Alistair Darling on advice from King (*The Crunch*, p. 77). King's views on the implications for competition policy of the Lloyds TSB–HBOS merger agreed in late 2008 are not publicly known.

16 Mervyn King, governor of the Bank of England, speech at the Northern Ireland Chamber of Commerce and Industry, Belfast, 9 October 2007, p. 6.

its balance-sheet totals – Northern Rock had *higher* unused inter-bank lines than Countrywide. Northern Rock's discussion of its own funding strategy also contained a sting in the tail, with the observation that 'Countrywide had the ability to use its mortgage backed notes as collateral to borrow from the US Federal Reserve … under a general liquidity facility available to all US banks, while Northern Rock was not able to borrow in the UK on the same basis, nor indeed through the ECB as it understands other UK banks with sizeable European operations were able to do'.[17]

King was wrong not just in his accusation against the Northern Rock management. More basically, he seemed not to have understood the purpose of central banking. Part of the trouble lay in differences in vocabulary and the gulf in thinking which these differences reflected. King's chosen phrase in his October 2007 speech, 'liquidity insurance', was a neologism in banking circles. Of course, all banking involves liquidity insurance if someone wants to put it like that. To the extent that banking gives customers an ability to make payments at future dates that they would not otherwise have, it insures them against unforeseen contingencies. So, when a bank extends an overdraft facility, the non-bank borrower can be said to have received 'liquidity insurance' or, when a bank agrees a line in the inter-bank market to another bank, the bank which may need to borrow can be regarded as a kind of policy-holder of 'liquidity insurance'. King's phrase is not, however, one that appears commonly in banking textbooks, or that bankers and their customers have ever favoured. Instead of saying that they pay 'premiums' for 'an

---

17 'Memorandum from Northern Rock', pp. Ev 231–9, section on 'Funding insurance', in House of Commons Treasury Committee, *The Run on the Rock*, 5th report of the 2007/08 session, The Stationery Office, London, 2008, vol. II.

insurance policy', they talk about 'arrangement' or 'commitment fees' for 'a line', 'a facility' or 'an overdraft'.[18]

But it was not King's choice of words which was the real problem. Banks can promise overdrafts to non-banks and one bank can pledge a line to other banks. In principle the proceeds of the overdraft can be converted into cash and an inter-bank line is available to cover a possible deficiency in a bank's balance at the central bank. But, ultimately, in modern circumstances no profit-seeking and privately owned commercial bank can produce one particular type of asset, legal-tender banknotes or 'cash' in its true sense. A private agent cannot promise to pay in cash unless it either already has the cash or is very certain that it can obtain cash in future; it certainly cannot create cash at nil cost, because that would break the legal tender laws: only one organisation can do so, namely the central bank.

If the entire system is short of cash, the existence of committed inter-bank lines for which arrangement fees have been paid may be no help. There is a high risk that banks will wriggle out of their commitments. When the whole system 'suffers from a lack of liquidity', banks will cancel as many inter-bank lines as possible without breaking contracts, and spreads and arrangement fees will increase. In that case the institution which – uniquely – can restore 'liquidity' is the central bank, since it is the only issuer of

18 The phrase 'liquidity insurance' was used in the Diamond and Dybvig article, cited in note 12 to Chapter 1, which seems to have been a major intellectual influence on King. It also appeared in the first sentence in an article by Graeme Chaplin et al., 'Banking system liquidity: developments and issues', on pp. 93–111 of the December 2000 issue of the Bank of England's *Financial Stability Review*. In the Chaplin article the phrase referred to the help given by banks to non-banks in making payments; in King's Belfast speech it referred to an inter-bank line. The meanings are quite distinct.

legal-tender notes. As far as the banks are concerned, they have a demand for the services of a central bank only because it will provide them with liquidity when they are short of cash. For the governor of a central bank to tell banks that they should provide liquidity insurance to each other, in order to pre-empt a crisis, is rather like a doctor telling a patient to leave the surgery because he should not have got ill in the first place. Either the central bank offers them 'liquidity insurance' to help them in a crisis or it is not a central bank.

Chapter 3 showed that banks could conduct all their usual business functions, including clearing, without a central bank. In the USA, before 1914, banks belonged to private clearing houses and these clearing houses issued liabilities that served as a means of settlement between their members. Such arrangements are inferior to central banking, but they are workable. Admittedly, the suggestion that British banks could withdraw their deposits from the Bank of England and switch their settlement business to a UK-based clearing house (with the clearing account in a large shareholder-owned bank) may sound implausible, even ridiculous, in today's conditions. To abandon settlement across a Bank of England account and instead to clear via a note exchange would certainly be expensive in resource terms. A different kind of exit from the Bank of England's jurisdiction, and from the mass of rules, regulations and controls enforced by the FSA, is, however, already a reality. In the modern world, where exchange controls have been abolished, banks can service large corporate customers from almost any commercial centre and in any currency. If the Bank of England will not provide useful services to British banks, they can relocate at least part of their activities to other countries where the central bank is more cooperative. There is nothing inevitable about the commitment of a certain sum of capital to a so-called 'British bank', obliged to lodge a deposit with the Bank of England, by a particular body of shareholders. The shareholders can up sticks, and move their capital and operations to a better location. This warning – that banks nowadays have a choice between at least three central banks (the US Fed, the ECB and the Bank of England) – was the sting in the tail in Northern Rock's evidence to the Treasury Committee.

No need to pre-fund deposit insurance

The Northern Rock affair was sad and pathetic, as well as unnecessary. It did, however, have an important redeeming feature. Despite the furore of late 2007, Northern Rock's depositors were able either to withdraw cash from their accounts or to switch the money to accounts at other banks. In that sense financial stability was maintained. Whether or not taxpayers eventually lose money because of the Northern Rock rescue is uncertain, but the latest news at the time of writing (November 2008) is fairly reassuring.[19] Until now the British banking system has not pre-funded a deposit insurance fund on a big scale. (It has paid premiums to a deposit insurance fund, but it has not committed a large capital sum.) On the evidence the Northern Rock affair has had one good outcome. This is to show that a large last-resort loan to a solvent bank can by itself protect depositors' interests and that the involvement of a deposit insurance agency, with a back-up fund, is unnecessary.

19　In its published accounts in mid-2008 Northern Rock continued to have positive shareholders' funds, despite a large charge against future bad debts. The bank's relatively good financial position was the more remarkable given that the fall in house prices between August 2007 and June 2008 was the largest in a ten-month period in British history.

But that is not how King saw the matter. Instead, as noted in Chapter 1, he urged that a deposit insurance system must be pre-funded and even described pre-funding as 'natural'. For anyone accustomed to banking, with its creation and cancellation of balances 'by a stroke of the pen', there is nothing whatever natural about the pre-funding of deposit insurance. On the contrary, the great achievement of banking is to have overcome the pot-of-banknotes fallacy and made the pre-funding of contingent future payments unnatural. Indeed, all the financial institutions of the modern world are man-made and artificial, and virtually all of them involve credit. None of them is 'natural', whatever that means, while credit implies the carrying-out of a transaction *before* payment. For King to demand payment *in advance* is to misunderstand what banking is all about.

In any case, it is obvious that, as long as all regulated banks are solvent, both a deposit insurance agency and a deposit insurance fund are superfluous, and pre-funding does not need to be discussed at all. For most of the last century the solvency of British banks has not been in question and deposit insurance has not existed. A deposit insurance fund is needed only when a bank is indeed bust because the lender of last resort facility provides liquidity for solvent banks.

But, even where a bank is bust, pre-funding of deposit insurance is not necessary. Suppose that the bust bank's capital deficiency exhausts the deposit insurance fund. In those circumstances the central bank can extend a loan to the deposit insurance fund, which can then pay out cash to depositors, and the deposit insurance fund can ask the commercial banks for money to repay the loan. Arrangements in which banks offer 'callable capital' in this way are more flexible and cheaper for the banking system than pre-funding. Of course, such arrangements ought to be on a contractual basis agreed well in advance of any crisis, but only an advance contractual commitment – not pre-funding – is necessary.

How is 'moral hazard' relevant?

King has one phrase that he uses repeatedly to justify his criticisms of traditional practices in British banking. The relevance of this phrase 'moral hazard' arises from the supposed danger that banks will choose risky assets if the Bank of England is a soft touch towards last-resort lending, rules on collateral, capital requirements and so on. King is right that the central bank's criteria for lending can affect banks' asset selection, as discussed in the section on loan collateral in Chapter 5. But the notion of 'moral hazard' has usually had a very different application in banking theory. This is the relevance of the deposit insurance system to the amount of care that potential depositors pay to banks' risk profiles. If deposits are fully insured (so that depositors will receive their cash back, come hell or high water), depositors have no incentive to check that banks are choosing safe assets; if deposits are less than fully insured, they have an incentive to monitor banks' asset holdings; and, if deposits are not insured at all, that incentive is very strong since – in the extreme – they could lose all their deposits. It follows that moral hazard in banking, the risk that banks will be reckless in their asset choice and business conduct, *increases* with the comprehensiveness of deposit insurance coverage. The more extensive and generous the deposit insurance given to banks' customers, the more likely it is that banks will select high-risk assets.

This lesson is a commonplace of the large literature on deposit insurance in the USA. Indeed, the history of deposit insurance as an institution says much about its disadvantages. Until the 1930s most banking regulation in the USA was at the state level and large numbers of state-specific deposit insurance funds were established at one time or another. Unfortunately, financial crises were often accompanied by widespread bank failures which exhausted the deposit insurance funds. Deposit insurance therefore had a mediocre reputation in the USA when the Federal Deposit Insurance Corporation was created in 1934.[20] The apparent success of the FDIC over the next 45 years may have been largely due to the high proportion of banks' assets in safe government securities, which reflected both the budget deficits of World War II and tight financial regulation, rather than the intrinsic merits of deposit insurance.

But in the 1970s and 1980s American banks increased their loans to the US private sector and to foreign governments, which raised the probabilities that their assets would suffer defaults. Since then academics and FDIC staff have written numerous books and papers on the moral hazard arising from deposit insurance. The message from this body of work is consistent: deposit insurance causes banks to take more risks. According to Professor Ed Kane in his *The Gathering Crisis in Federal Deposit Insurance*, which was published in 1985, 'Conflicts between the interests of the two parties to an insurance contract mean that, like acrobats working with the benefit of a safety net, insureds can afford to

---

20 Westerfield, *Money, Credit and Banking*, Ronald Press, New York, 1938, p. 969. See also Charles Calomiris and Eugene White, 'The origins of federal deposit insurance', in Calomiris, *US Bank Deregulation in Historical Perspective*, Cambridge University Press, Cambridge and New York, 2000, pp. 164–211.

be more daring than they could if they were not able to rely on insurance coverage to truncate their losses.' In his view the FDIC ought to restrict excessive risk-taking by bankers, but the FDIC was subject to political pressure to avoid restrictions and indeed to favour such risky lending practices as mortgage lending to low-income households. Kane even referred to 'the deposit-insurance subsidy to risk-taking', which increases 'the fragility of our financial system'.[21] Kane's conclusion was not new. In the 1930s a textbook on American banking noted that the most telling argument against deposit insurance was that it put all bankers 'on the same level, making the deposits in new, inexperienced, reckless, or dishonest banks as safe as deposits in old, proved, conservative and honest banks'.[22]

King has emphasised the moral hazard supposedly implicit in last-resort lending by the central bank and urged an expansion of deposit insurance. The truth is that commercial banks do everything they can to avoid last-resort borrowing, which is expensive and humiliating, and usually ends the careers of the executives initiating it. By contrast, decades of experience in the USA show that deposit insurance tends to encourage excessive and improper risk-taking by banks. The phrase 'moral hazard' ought to be associated with deposit insurance, not with last-resort lending.

King's philosophy of central banking

The last few paragraphs have been highly critical both of the latest

---

21 Edward J. Kane, *The Gathering Crisis in Federal Deposit Insurance*, MIT Press, Cambridge, MA, 1985, pp. 145–6. The quotation earlier in the text comes from pp. 14–15.
22 Westerfield, op. cit., p. 980.

trends in public policy towards the British banking industry and, in particular, of arguments and proposals made by the current governor of the Bank of England, Mervyn King. But King is far from alone in his views. Indeed, he can appeal to a substantial body of doctrine in his support. He can be seen as the most prominent current representative of a distinguished school of thought which goes back almost two hundred years. This school will be labelled 'the Currency School' in order to take the discussion forward, although readers should be warned that the real-world Currency School of early Victorian times was more subtle than is being suggested here.

A key tenet of the Currency School is that the central bank should not lend to the private sector at all. According to its originators in the early nineteenth century, money issuance is of two very different kinds, notes and deposits. Experience has shown that people value uniformity and reliability in their notes, so that the universal long-run trend has been for notes to be issued by only one institution (the central bank) and to have legal-tender status.[23] Given the special nature of the legal-tender note issue, the Currency School recommends that the central bank's assets should consist either of so-called 'hard assets', such as gold and silver, or of claims on the government. It follows that the central bank, the bank of issue, should not demean itself by transacting with any private sector agent. An obvious extension of this line of thought is that the central bank has no responsibility to lend to a bank suffering from a lack of liquidity and so should not be a

---

23   This proposition is denied by many members of the Free Banking school. Larry White, a supporter of free banking, has argued, however, that 'a unit of account emerges wedded to a general medium of exchange'. Lawrence H. White, 'Competitive payments systems and the unit of account', *American Economic Review*, 74(4), 1984, pp. 699–712: the quotation is from p. 711.

lender of last resort. The Currency School's attitude towards the second type of money, the bank deposit, is dismissive. Deposits are of course issued by privately owned commercial banks subject to an assortment of motives, of which profit maximisation is the most important. Bank deposits are supposed to be convertible into notes, but – according to at least one version of the Currency School – the preservation of that convertibility is a matter for the private sector and should not be of concern to the note-issuing central bank. By extension, the banking system is of no more interest to economic policymakers than, say, the car industry or food manufacturing.[24]

Perhaps the earliest statement of this set of views was by David Ricardo in his pamphlet *Plan for a National Bank*, which was published in 1824 shortly after his death. He advocated that the note-issuing function of the Bank of England should be trans-ferred to a newly created National Bank, where the notes were to be fully collateralised by bullion. The National Bank would maintain the government's account and so act as banker to the government, but – unlike the Bank of England – it would not lend to any private sector corporation or individual.[25] Ricardo's pamphlet was republished in 1838 and must have been a major influence on the 1844 Bank Charter Act. The 1844 Act did not establish a new national bank, but it split the Bank of England into

24 The Currency School is an intellectual ancestor of New Classical Economics. In a well-known 1980 article on 'Banking in a theory of finance', one of the leaders of New Classical thinking, Eugene Fama, denied that the banking system has any particular significance for the economy's general equilibrium. E. Fama, 'Banking in a theory of finance', *Journal of Monetary Economics*, 6, 1980, pp. 39–57.

25 Ricardo's proposals for a National Bank are presented at various points in Piero Sraffa (ed.), *The Works and Correspondence of David Ricardo*, vol. V: *Speeches and Evidence*, Cambridge University Press for the Royal Economic Society, Cambridge, 1952.

two. The job of the Issue Department was to issue legal-tender notes against the backing of bullion in the Bank's vaults, with only a small unbacked 'fiduciary issue'; the task of the Banking Department was to lend money like other banks and make a profit for the shareholders. In substance the Issue Department was Ricardo's National Bank.

The same underlying thinking has resurfaced on several occasions and taken a variety of forms. In 1935 Irving Fisher advocated what he called '100% Money' in a book of that name. The heart of the proposal was that banks' sight deposits should be fully backed by legal-tender notes. Since the state could control the volume of legal-tender notes, the 100 per cent cash reserve requirement would enable it also to control the level of sight deposits. When Fisher was writing some economists believed that 'money' consisted of the public's note holdings and their sight deposits with the banks, and that time deposits were not properly 'money'; indeed, many economists still hold this belief.[26] For them Fisher's 100 per cent money proposal had an important merit, that it would end private sector banks' ability to create new money balances by extending credit. Fisher believed in a monetary theory of the business cycle, and was confident that 100 per cent money would end booms and depressions. In his words, 'This 100 per cent plan is the only plan that would absolutely separate the control of money from banking.'[27] So, as with Ricardo in 1824, the creation of those assets that are genuinely 'money' is to lie entirely

26 See, for example, Allan Meltzer's tendency to equate M1 (which excludes time deposits) with 'the money supply' in his *A History of the Federal Reserve*, University of Chicago Press, Chicago, 2003.

27 William J. Barber (ed.), *The Works of Irving Fisher*, vol. 11: *100% Money*, Pickering & Chatto, London, 1997 (originally published in 1935 by the Adelphi Company of New York), p. 7.

with the state. Not only should the business of banking be entirely separate from money creation, but the private sector's allegedly dangerous ability to create money balances must be outlawed.

The latest expression of these ideas has come from proponents of so-called 'narrow banking'. Narrow banking comes to much the same thing as Fisher's 100 per cent plan, although with a range of nuances. Sometimes the proposal is that *all* bank liabilities must be matched with cash or with a mixture of cash and government securities, and that credit should no longer be extended by 'banks', but instead by distinct 'finance companies'. It needs to be emphasised that, although these notions strike at the institutional foundations of a contemporary market economy, their supporters are not mavericks. Maurice Allais, the French economist who won the Nobel Prize in 1988, has said, 'In essence the present creation of money out of nothing by the banking system is similar to the creation of money by counterfeiters, so rightly condemned by the law.'[28] Milton Friedman and James Tobin, also winners of the Nobel Prize for economics, both wrote articles sympathetic to the 100 per cent reserves principle, although these articles do not seem to have become their settled verdicts on the question.[29]

Is there an affinity between these ideas – the ideas that began with the Currency School in early-nineteenth-century Britain – and recent statements from Mervyn King? As already noted, in several of these statements King has expressed an obvious distaste for Bank of England lending to any private sector

---

28 The author has been unable to obtain the original source for this quotation, which appears in Allais's Wikipedia entry.

29 For Friedman, see 'A monetary and fiscal framework for monetary stability', *American Economic Review*, 38(3), 1948, pp. 245–64; for Tobin, see 'Financial innovation and deregulation in perspective', *Bank of Japan Monetary and Economic Studies*, 3, 1985, pp. 19–29.

organisation. He is willing for the Bank to engage in repo transactions with commercial banks, since such transactions envisage
early cash repayment at an agreed rate. Indeed, if the Bank were
not to engage in such transactions, it could not set the short-
term interest rate that King certainly regards as key to the Bank's
delivery of monetary stability.

But King has been opposed to more meaningful loans, loans
that may last over an extended period, imply an element of nego-
tiation about the terms and carry the possibility, however faint,
that the Bank of England would not get its money back. That is
certainly an interpretation allowed by his attitude towards Lloyds
TSB's request for a facility to further its possible acquisition of
Northern Rock in the summer of 2007. It is further confirmed
both by the Bank's eagerness to shunt the Northern Rock loan
off its balance sheet and hand it over to the Treasury, and by
further remarks from King on 11 September 2008 (to the Treasury
Committee of the House of Commons) in which he said that it
had never been a central bank's job to provide long-term loans
to banks. He claimed that only private savers or taxpayers via the
government could provide such funds.[30]

King's statement is plain wrong. As a logical matter, if
commercial banks are able to provide long-term inter-bank
lines to each other (and they certainly can do this), the central
bank must also be able to extend long-term loans to banks. As a
matter of fact, the Bank of England has on numerous instances
extended loans to privately owned banks which have either had an

---

30   King's claim is contradicted by numerous examples in the Bank's own history.
     For example, in the early 1930s Lazards received a large loan which lasted for sev-
     eral years; Richard Sayers, *The Bank of England 1891–1944*, Cambridge University
     Press, Cambridge, 1976, p. 532.

eventual term of several years or have been so regularly renewed that their effective terms have in fact been several years. (See the discussion of the duration of last-resort facilities in Chapter 5.) In sharp contrast to King's position, Ben Bernanke, chairman of the USA's Federal Reserve, said in August 2008, 'Unless I hear from Congress that I should not be responding to a crisis situation, I think that it's a long-standing role of the central bank to use its lender-of-last-resort facilities.'[31] Without doubt many of the loans extended by the Federal Reserve in 2008 will last for several years.

Is it going too far to suggest that King wants the Bank of England to drop the lender-of-last-resort role? Is his vision of a central bank that it should be restricted to the setting of interest rates and the attainment of monetary stability, with the job of maintaining financial stability given to other agencies? And would not this model of the Bank of England's role reduce it to not much more than a large-scale economic research department?

Chapters 3 to 5 of this study argued that central banking allowed banks to reduce their ratios of cash and capital to their assets, and so lowered the cost of finance to non-banks, but that these benefits could be enjoyed only if the central bank had a lender-of-last-resort function. The present trend in British public policy is away from this conception of the relationship between commercial banks and the central bank, and instead towards King's model of the central bank as economic research department. This trend is misguided and must be resisted. Nevertheless, it is important to understand that King's attitudes towards the subject have much in common with those discussed approvingly by figures like Ricardo, Irving Fisher, Maurice Allais, Tobin and

---

31 Quotation from 'Hire the A-Team', *The Economist*, 9 August 2008, p. 66.

even Milton Friedman. King could be regarded as the most recent of a long line of influential representatives of the Currency School tradition.

7 HOW SHOULD THE BANK OF ENGLAND BE ORGANISED?

If the question were asked 'what went wrong in the Northern Rock affair and the subsequent banking crisis?', the answer would have to be 'almost everything'. The key players in British officialdom committed blunder after blunder. Serious mistakes in banking policy – such as regulators' failure to manufacture sufficient liquid assets for the banks (described at the start of Chapter 6) – had been made in previous years. Nevertheless, in early 2007 British banks were profitable and solvent, and had complied with regulations. In August and September 2007 the breakdown in the wholesale money markets left a handful of UK specialist mortgage banks, including Northern Rock, badly placed. While their managements had been too ambitious, their condition ought not to have been terminal. Difficult negotiations about their fate, and about banking regulation in the large, were needed between the UK banking system on the one hand and the Tripartite Authorities on the other. But these should have been private and low-key, and should have been kept out of the headlines and the wider political debate. There was no need for a huge quarrel leading to the slashing of banks' market capitalisation by tens of billions of pounds and a severe downturn in economic activity. The contrast between the Bank of England's successful handling of the secondary banking crisis in the mid-1970s and the small banks crisis in the early 1990s, and the Tripartite Authorities' (and particularly the Bank of England's) handling of the banking traumas of 2007 and 2008, could hardly be more extreme.

Had the banks cut their cash and liquidity too much?

But the actions of individuals must always be set within a larger institutional and historical context, and in many respects the recent turmoil in British banking (and of course in banking elsewhere) was an accident waiting to happen. The six decades from the end of World War II had been characterised by gradual but relentless measures towards the liberalisation of banking systems from government restrictions, as well as by the globalisation of both finance and its regulation. The Bank of England – like other central banks – had allowed banks to economise on their cash and liquid asset holdings to an extent that would have been considered astonishing in the early post-war years. The UK's commercial banks believed that the skimpiness of the cash on their balance sheets was not particularly risky. In the middle years of the current decade they complied with the Basel rules on solvency, while their relations with both the FSA and the Bank were cordial.

The implicit assumption was that – as long as their businesses had adequate capital and their assets were of good quality – the Bank of England would readily exchange part of their assets for cash, probably on first-resort terms but on last-resort terms if necessary. Their low holdings of cash and liquid assets ought therefore not to cause serious trouble. As noted in Chapter 5, this assumption became untenable in August and September 2007 because of King's initial refusal to ease collateral requirements in repo operations, Darling's decision (on King's advice) to block the Northern Rock–Lloyds TSB takeover attempt and by the run on Northern Rock which soon followed. (Of course, the recent banking crisis has been global in impact. But regulatory trends in other countries have been similar to those in the UK and it serves the immediate argument to focus on the UK.)

King worked in tandem with Alistair Darling, the Chancellor of the Exchequer, in the crisis period. As both men were aware, the Bank of England was constrained by the small size of its capital, which was under £2 billion. If the Bank of England lent £30 billion to Northern Rock, if Northern Rock was unable to repay the loan and if the shortfall were, say, £3 billion, the Bank of England would be 'bust'. As the bankrupting of the Bank of England would be an apparently cataclysmic event, King had to make sure that he had an indemnity against loss for any large loan that his institution extended.[1] That indemnity could come only from the Bank's shareholder, the government itself, and would require a legal contract between the Bank and the Treasury. In any negotiations the Treasury would be 'in the driving seat'. The Bank's low capitalisation and consequent vulnerability to loss on assets of any kind, along with his Currency School views, made King nervous about last-resort lending. He clearly favoured the transfer of his organisation's banking functions to either the Treasury or to entirely new agencies with no track record whatsoever.

The Treasury, however, employed few people with any meaningful banking experience, and key officials and ministers regarded last-resort lending as an abuse of 'government money'.[2]

---

1   Alex Brummer, *The Crunch*, Random House, London, 2008, p. 77.
2   In the legal action that followed the nationalisation of Northern Rock, Mr John Kingman – the second permanent secretary at the Treasury in charge of the nationalisation exercise – proposed a new doctrine. This was that, because 'government money' had been 'injected' into Northern Rock, a proper 'return' should

The details of the banking system's cash operations and capital rules, which are technical subjects of great complexity, became politicised. Public discussion of banking regulation favoured the reinforcement of deposit insurance and an attenuation of the Bank of England's lender-of-last-resort role, despite the mixed international record of deposit insurance schemes and the irrelevance of such arrangements in a world where all banks are solvent. Whereas King has claimed that central bank lending on terms that were too easy may cause moral hazard in banks' asset selection, a large academic literature backed up by decades of practical experience emphasises that deposit insurance systems increase moral hazard on the part of depositors and are a menace to responsible banking.

What must be done to restore good relations between the state and Britain's banks, and to re-establish a healthy financial system?

---

be earned on that money, if necessary at the expense of the shareholders. It was claimed that the loan was risky and involved 'public subsidy', even though it was provided at above-market rates. It was then proposed that the state could appropriate a return, over and above the interest due on the loan, to compensate for the alleged risk (witness statement of John Kingman, in action between Northern Rock claimants and HM Treasury, 31 July 2008, clause 139). The question of how this 'return' was to be determined, and whether it would be valid if it did not arise from a prior contractual arrangement voluntarily reached between Northern Rock and the Tripartite Authorities, raised fundamental uncertainties about the property rights of Northern Rock shareholders. These uncertainties, which must now worry any potential investor in the UK banking system, had never arisen in previous last-resort episodes in which the Bank of England had been operating more or less autonomously from the Treasury.

How should the Bank of England organise its lending activity?

Chapter 5 reviewed the lender-of-last-resort function in some detail. The present discussion needs only to complement that review in the light of the Northern Rock affair and its sequel. The first point can hardly be controversial, that relationships between the Bank of England and the commercial banks suffered severely from a lack of contractual certainty. In the summer of 2007 the banks had no legal justification for believing that the Bank of England would accept mortgage-backed assets in repo operations. But they did have good reasons, arising from experience and practice over many decades, for expecting the Bank to be lenient in difficult conditions. Some bankers could remember the acute money market shortage which followed the UK's expulsion from the European Exchange Rate Mechanism in September 1992, when the Bank had without fuss taken a huge range of assets in overnight repo activity.

As noted in Chapter 3, a core proposal in the Bank of England's 2006 Red Book on money market operations was that so-called 'settlement banks' should have the unlimited capacity to borrow against eligible collateral.[3] On 26 October 2006, Ian Bond, the Bank's head of financial crisis management, gave a workshop presentation to the British Bankers Association which, in the light of later events, might be described as offering a false prospectus. Bond said that banks' unlimited capacity to borrow was to be usually at a penalty rate, but not always. In fact, 'Following major operational or financial disruption, we can reduce the penalty

---

3   The phrase 'settlement banks' included both the clearing banks and a number of non-clearing banks which, because of changes in technology, carried out extensive settlement business. See footnote 19 on page 60 above.

– if necessary, to the point at which we are lending at Bank Rate.' The thinking was that this would 'reduce the risk of a short-term liquidity problem developing into a full-blown crisis'.[4]

When a liquidity problem arose in August 2007, the Bank was less obliging. Instead of preventing a full-blown crisis, the Bank's actions were largely responsible for causing one. King's hard-line attitude towards government securities as repo collateral and the payment of a penalty rate in standing facilities practically disowned the remarks made by a senior Bank official, in an open forum with many bankers present, less than a year earlier. As the last chapter showed, in the late summer of 2007 the Bank of England undoubtedly broke the spirit of Bagehot's rules. Bagehot was right to complain in *Lombard Street* in the 1870s that the lender-of-last-resort function was 'unimposed, unacknowledged and denied'. In the early 21st century that function must now be acknowledged and spelt out in a legally binding contract. The doctrine of 'constructive ambiguity' is hocus-pocus and has failed.[5]

4   Ian Bond, 'Managing a bank-specific crisis: a UK perspective' (mimeo), BBA workshop presentation, 26 October 2006, Bank of England, London, pp. 4–5.

5   On 2 April 2008 Paul Tucker, the Bank of England's executive director for markets, gave a speech on 'Monetary policy and the financial system', in which he said, 'a Social Contract between the banking system and the authorities', in which banks could borrow on last-resort terms if they had a cash problem, had been in place 'for well over a century'. But he judged that since the summer of 2007 it had been 'toxic' for banks to borrow from the central bank, in the way suggested by the contract (see the article in *Bank of England Quarterly Bulletin*, 2008 Q2 issue, 48(2), p. 205). He did not specify, however, whether a legally binding contract and 'a Social Contract' came to the same thing.

Repurchase activity and other types of asset acquisition

Chapter 5 distinguished between first-resort and last-resort loans, between cash provided to banks on a repurchase basis with a clearly specified payback date and amount, and cash provided with some uncertainty, even if very slight, about repayment. A further distinction now needs to be developed. The central bank can inject cash into the banking system not by making a loan or buying assets on a repo basis, but by purchasing assets outright. Indeed, the dominance of repo arrangements in the Bank of England's open market operations is a recent development which began in the 1990s, at least partly as a by-product of the UK's expected adhesion to the European single currency project. Outright purchases by the Bank were the historical norm in the relief of cash shortages. Of course, one effect of such purchases is that the Bank assumes the risk of default on any assets it acquires. The Bank must therefore pay attention to the quality of these assets and needs to discuss with the commercial banks the asset types that are eligible. As explained early in Chapter 6, such discussions were a constant feature of the interaction between the Bank and the UK's banking system until the end of the twentieth century.

The contemporary focus on repo transactions is appropriate if the central bank's task is deemed solely to be the setting of an interest rate to keep inflation in line with its target. It is appropriate, in other words, if the central bank is concerned only with monetary stability. But – as emphasised throughout this monograph – financial stability is also a recognised part of a typical central bank's remit. In a repo transaction a commercial bank receives cash in exchange for an asset, but agrees to hand back that cash at a relatively early date (usually only a few weeks) when the asset returns to its own balance sheet. The bank does own extra cash, but only on a temporary and provisional basis. By contrast, when the central bank buys assets outright from a commercial bank, that commercial bank owns the cash, full stop. The question needs to be asked, 'if the entire banking system has inadequate cash, perhaps with the shortage manifesting itself by high inter-bank rates, which type of central bank deal – the repo transaction or the outright asset purchase – is likely to be more effective in eliminating the shortage?' The answer surely is that outright purchases are almost certain to be better.[6] The cash held by a bank from a repo agreement has to be paid back fairly quickly to the central bank, whereas the cash arising from an asset sale (i.e. a permanent sale to the central bank) has to be put to work elsewhere in the banking system or perhaps even loaned out to non-banks. Of course, when a bank flush with cash seeks to place it with another bank, then that expands the inter-bank market. Repos can create an excess supply of cash in the banking system only if conducted on an immense scale and perhaps not even then; direct asset purchases ought to be able to establish an excess supply of cash with little difficulty.[7]

6   The truth of this observation is demonstrated by the huge expansion of the Bank of England's balance sheet that followed the adoption of repo as the main type of open-market operation in the late 1990s. This expansion had no clear effect in narrowing the differential between the policy rate and the inter-bank rate, except in the overnight market.

7   This statement assumes that a meaningful positive extra return is available on assets other than a commercial bank's balance at the central bank. In Japan in the late 1990s and early years of the present century banks had enormous balances at the Bank of Japan, but did not behave as if they had an excess supply of cash (they were constrained to some extent by lack of capital). The author advocated the resumption of occasional outright asset purchases by the Bank of England in an article, written jointly with Brandon Davies, on 'A simple plan to unclog the interbank market', *Financial Times*, 22 October 2008.

Late 2007 and 2008 were marked by a breakdown in the UK inter-bank and wholesale money markets, and a large differential between the Bank's policy rate and inter-bank rates. The problems were international in scope and stemmed to a considerable extent from mistrust between banks, as they doubted each other's solvency. But the blockages in the inter-bank market were also partly attributable to central banks' excessive reliance on repo operations and their hesitation in making genuine asset purchases from the commercial banks. Indeed, it was striking that banks' large capital-raising efforts appeared to make little impression on the differentials between the policy rate and inter-bank rates. The message is that central banks – including the Bank of England – must again be prepared to conduct large outright asset transactions with commercial banks, with the intention of altering the amount of cash truly in commercial banks' ownership. This has significant implications for central bank organisation, to which the discussion will return in the next section. But a related point may now be inserted into the discussion.

It was shown in Chapter 3 that banks have a functional requirement to hold cash to meet deposit withdrawals in their branch networks and obligations to settle debts with other banks. Banks' demand to hold cash is partly a matter of technology and institutions, but – from time to time – their equilibrium ratio of cash to assets may be boosted by fears that counterparties in the settlement system (i.e. banks, mostly) are unable to meet their commitments. Further, these fears may spread to the non-bank public, who can be worried (as the Northern Rock affair showed) that they 'will not get their money back'. The non-bank public therefore also comes to have a higher equilibrium ratio of cash to deposits. Suppose that the central bank is confident that all the settlement banks are solvent, that the banking system is sound and that the fears are (in Roosevelt's words in the closing phase of the USA's Great Depression) 'of fear itself'. Then it must react by increasing banks' cash holdings so that the ratio of cash to assets rises to the new equilibrium level and banks do not shrink assets.

If banks shrink assets, their liabilities must fall. Since banks' liabilities are dominated by deposits, and since deposits constitute most of the quantity of money, a major decline in banks' assets is virtually certain to lead to a drop in the quantity of money. If the quantity of money falls, damaging impacts on output and employment are almost inevitable, and in the extreme a self-reinforcing process of so-called 'debt deflation' may be initiated.[8] It follows that, in emergency conditions, the central bank must accommodate changes in the equilibrium ratio of cash to deposits, in order to keep the quantity of money and wider macroeconomic conditions fairly stable. The principle is recognised as good practice in most treatises on central banking. According to Humphrey, 'The result [of a panic] is a massive rise in the demand for base money – a rise that, if not satisfied by increased issues, produces sharp contractions in the money stock and equally sharp contractions in spending ... [T]he lender of last resort must be prepared to offset falls in the money multiplier arising from panic-induced rises in currency and reserve ratios with compensating rises in the monetary base.'[9] In the Great Depression in the USA, and in the 1990s in Japan, the central bank balance sheet rose enormously

---

8   The classic statement of the debt-deflation process was in a 1933 Irving Fisher article, 'The debt-deflation theory of great depressions', *Econometrica*, 1, 1933, pp. 337–57. Fisher's account of the process assumed a monetary theory of the determination of national income.

9   Thomas M. Humphrey, *Money, Banking and Inflation*, Edward Elgar, Aldershot and Brookfield, USA, 1993, p. 16.

relative to GDP, largely to counterbalance the effect of falls in the money multiplier on the quantity of money.

The central bank must have strong capital resources

The argument of the last section was that, from time to time and certainly when a run is threatened or under way, the central bank should have the ability to purchase assets outright (which adds risk), and to expand its balance sheet quickly and perhaps very significantly (which also adds risk). The extra risks fall on the central bank's capital. A key conclusion follows from this: if the central bank is – by itself, without the support of another agency of the state – to play a substantive role in maintaining financial stability, it must have capital resources strong enough to handle a major crisis. The quantification of the central bank's optimal capital requirement is an interesting and quite new subject, to which no settled body of theory relates. One line of approach would be to suggest that central banks should hold capital equal to some fraction of the banking system's balance sheet total and/ or nominal GDP. Further, if over a period of several years the central bank's capital has declined relative to either variable, its ability to perform a lender-of-last-resort role is likely to be impaired.

At their foundation central banks were usually very large relative to the rest of the banking system. In Britain, for example, the Bank of England was by far the largest banking institution throughout the eighteenth century and remained so until the late nineteenth century. The doctrine that the Bank of England should act as lender of last resort developed when it was a heavyweight organisation, in terms of capital and hence of its ability to add assets. This remained true, although to a lesser extent, during the first three quarters of the twentieth century. At the end of 1973, just ahead of the secondary banking crisis of 1974–76, the Bank of England's capital was over £300 million, while the non-deposit liabilities (which would have been mostly capital) of the London and Scottish clearing banks were just under £850 million.[10] The Bank of England launched the 'lifeboat', asking the clearing banks to accept possible losses for the greater good of the system. The clearing banks agreed to perform this role, but – not surprisingly – they wanted the burden shared with the Bank of England. In a meeting on 27 December 1973, between the clearing bank chiefs, led by Sir Eric Faulkner of Lloyds Bank, and the governor and deputy governor of the Bank of England, the Bank said that it would cover 10 per cent of any losses in the support operation.[11] With the total of inter-bank loans in the lifeboat scheme estimated to have reached £1.3 billion, it seems that the Bank drove a hard bargain. As it happens, final losses on the lifeboat itself were negligible, although the Bank had heavy losses in a distinct support operation for Slater Walker Securities. But the Bank evidently could have absorbed a loss of £50 million or so phased over a few years, without extreme political embarrassment. According to Reid, who analysed the Bank's annual reports and accounts in the relevant period, the losses totalled about £100 million.[12]

The numbers may seem small by today's standards, but it needs to be remembered that national income has risen manyfold since the early 1970s. With nominal GDP in 1973 at £74.0 billion,

---

10   *Bank of England Quarterly Bulletin*, Bank of England, London, June 1974, Tables 5, 8/2 and 8/3.

11   Margaret Reid, *The Secondary Banking Crisis*, Macmillan, London, 1982, p. 16.

12   Ibid., pp. 190–91.

Figure 5   **How much capital do the Bank of England and UK banks have?**
Ratio of Bank of England's capital to non-deposit liabilities
(mostly equity and bond capital) of UK banking system, %

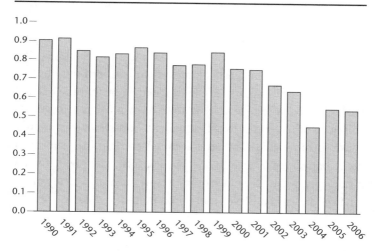

At end-2006 the Bank of England's capital of just under £1.9 billion was little more than 0.5% of the combined equity and bond capital of the UK banking system.

the Bank of England's capital of £300 million was about 0.4 per cent of GDP. The Bank's capital in the early 21st century would bear the same relationship with GDP if it approximated to £6 billion. In fact, the number is little more than £2 billion. The contrast between the Bank's capital strength today and 35 years ago is even more extreme if the comparator is the balance-sheet size (and so the potential risk) of the UK's banking system, since banks have grown faster than GDP almost continuously over the last 25 years. In February 2007 the Bank's capital was £1.86 billion, while the UK banking system's sterling non-deposit liabilities (which would have been largely equity and bond capital) amounted to £346.9 billion. Whereas in 1973 the Bank's own capital resources were about a third of those of the clearing banks, which were dominant players in the commercial banking system, at present they are a mere 0.5 per cent of all UK banks' total capital. As Figure 5 shows, the decline in the Bank's capital relative to that of the UK banking system has been unremitting over the last fifteen years. The message must be that the Bank of England's ability to take risks on to to its own balance sheet – its ability, in other words, to act as lender of last resort – is severely constrained relative to a quite recent past within the memory of many bankers still alive today. The contrast with the situation historically, when the lender-of-last-resort role was evolving in the nineteenth century, is even more pronounced.

The case for privatising the Bank of England

Some financial commentators might object that the meagreness of the Bank of England's capital is of no importance. The Bank of England is owned by the state and is accountable to the Treasury. At the end of the day it has the full fiscal resources of the British government behind it. As long as the Treasury endorses its decisions, it can therefore expand or contract its balance sheet at will. In any case, because it is in public ownership, it cannot at present make substantial last-resort loans without the Treasury's approval. On this view a call for the expansion of the Bank of England's capital appears to misunderstand its constitutional position and to be a red herring.

Here we come to perhaps the most controversial proposal in this chapter. Not only should the Bank of England have the capital to act freely and efficiently as a large-scale lender of last resort, but also it should be privatised. Two strong arguments for privatisation emerged from the banking crisis of 2007 and 2008. First, the Bank's lack of financial resources obliged it throughout the crisis to confer with – and invariably to defer to – the Treasury. Although this had been implicit in its constitutional status since nationalisation in 1946, the Bank operated with a fair degree of autonomy from the Treasury in the first big post-war crisis in the 1970s. In Reid's words in her classic account of *The Secondary Banking Crisis*,

> It is a long-standing joke, not quite unconnected with
> genuine rivalry, that the Treasury sees the Bank of England
> as its 'East End branch', while it is itself, of course, regarded
> by the Bank as its 'West End branch'. There is no doubt that,
> in the response to the fringe banking crisis, the decision-
> making rested overwhelmingly at the east end of the axis.[13]

By contrast, in the Northern Rock affair the Treasury's officials were more salient at key meetings than those of the Bank of England, largely because the Treasury pulled the purse strings. This might not have mattered if Treasury civil servants had had a good grasp of banking realities, but their banking knowledge and experience were usually negligible.[14]

---

13   Ibid., p. 19.

14   John Kingman was the Treasury civil servant in charge of the Northern Rock negotiations in late 2007. His career since leaving Oxford in 1991 had been mostly
at the Treasury, with no time in banking and finance apart from a directorship of
the non-commercial European Investment Bank. Newspaper stories reported on
his friendship with Robert Peston, the BBC journalist who had a series of 'scoops'
on official policy towards the banking system, starting with that which caused
the run on Northern Rock in September 2007: see, for example, Christopher
Leake, 'BBC man's intriguing web of friendships behind the scoop that shocked
the banking world', *Mail on Sunday*, 12 October 2008.

The setting of deadlines for early repayment of Northern Rock's last-resort loan was a particular folly. In previous last-resort episodes the Bank, working largely by itself, had not hurried the repayment of its support facilities, but instead had given the borrowing bank time to reorganise its affairs and so to achieve the highest return from its assets. But, on 28 September 2007, the Treasury sought the European Commission's opinion on whether the British state's support of Northern Rock broke EU state aid rules. Such rules specified a six-month time limit on government help for a private sector business, unless certain criteria were satisfied. Since the Commission was expected to deem that the support was state aid (and in the end did so), the Treasury imposed on any investor in Northern Rock a require-ment that the last-resort loan be repaid within six months. This was wholly unrealistic and was a key reason why no private sector investor decided to buy the bank.[15] The pressure on Northern Rock for rapid repayment of the loan was also destructive in another sense, in that it both undermined the demand for housing and reduced the amount of money in the economy. Amazingly, in November 2008 – after more than half of the initial loan of almost £30 billion had been repaid – Darling became concerned that, in the words of the *Sunday Times*, Northern Rock's 'dash for cash has helped destabilise the UK's housing market'.[16] Had he not been the minister responsible in late 2007 for determining the timing of the loan's repayment?

The clumsiness of officialdom in the Northern Rock affair

---

15 One of the potential bidders for Northern Rock in late 2007 was the Olivant con-sortium. It wanted five years to repay the Bank of England loan. Brummer, op. cit., p. 171.

16 'Darling seeks delay on Rock repayment', *Sunday Times*, 16 November 2008.

contrasted with the Bank of England's adroit handling of particular cases not only in the secondary banking crisis, but also in the small banks crisis in the early 1990s. In the small banks crisis the Bank had often kept loan facilities in place for several years, whatever the EU's rules.[17] Central banking is best done by central bankers, not by civil servants from the finance ministry. But central bankers can take charge only if they have control over the financial levers. If the central bank were privately owned, a management appointed by shareholders – and not semi-retired civil servants overseen by supposed 'experts' with partisan attitudes and dependent on politicians' favour – would take the key decisions.

But the second and more fundamental justification for privatising the central bank is that any last-resort loans would then be from one private sector agent to another. Media prattle about 'government money' was a recurring theme throughout the banking crisis and hampered sensible discussion of the underlying issues. Many people seemed to think that the government was 'spending' money on Northern Rock and other British banks in the same way that it spent money on roads and hospitals. But

---

17   The European Commission's Decision, which appeared on 5 December 2007, specifically exempted a lender-of-last-resort loan from the EU's state aid rules. This may have been why no one thought to invoke these rules in the secondary banking crisis or the small banks crisis. The question raised is, 'why was the Treasury so keen to seek the Commission's verdict on the Northern Rock facilities?' The trouble was that the Northern Rock package included a state guarantee on its deposits as well as the loan from the Bank of England. The Commission's view was that, while a lender-of-last-resort loan is not in itself state aid, the deposit guarantees given to Northern Rock were state aid and that the six-month deadline did therefore apply. But when banks across the EU faced runs in the autumn of 2008 a number of governments extended deposit guarantees to their entire banking systems, without seeking the Commission's permission or bothering themselves about state aid rules.

a payment of money can have a wide variety of legal significations and the true meaning may need to be specified carefully. The lender-of-last-resort loan to Northern Rock was just that, a loan that had to be repaid. It was not a grant or an item of direct government expenditure; it was also not an injection of equity capital, on which the government was entitled to seek a return over and above the interest payments on the loan.[18] One of the most ugly consequences of the crisis has been the politicisation of banking, with all sorts of populist and irresponsible pressures on the banking industry. No doubt some of this would continue if the Bank of England were privately owned, but a privatised Bank of England would be better able to keep banking matters out of the public spotlight. Crucially, a loan from the Bank of England to a commercial bank could be viewed as another kind of inter-bank transaction, of interest not to the wider world of politics and the media, but only to the private parties involved

The capital of a privatised Bank of England

Which private agents would provide the Bank's capital? Fortunately, an example is already to hand, the Federal Reserve system in the USA. When the Fed was founded Congress was anxious that it might become a creature of the central government in Washington, which would encroach on the powers that remained at state level. So neither the federal government nor state governments became shareholders in the new organisation. Instead

---

18 The much-heard phrase 'an injection of government money' is a media simplification and has several meanings. See note 2 above for the use of this phrase to lead to the doctrine that 'the government should seek an extra return on its money', with the consequent threat to the property rights of banks' shareholders.

the capital was subscribed by member banks themselves. At the outset the subscription to the Fed was set at 6 per cent of member banks' own capital, a number which was criticised as 'arbitrary' and 'no more than a guess at what the capital requirements of the reserve banks would be'.[19] Nevertheless, the 6 per cent figure still applies. Half of it must be paid in, while the other half is subject to call by the Fed's board of governors.

Another approach to the topic would be to judge from the historical record the maximum size of central bank exposures during financial crises and to assess the implied requirement for capital. Until the recent troubles, UK experience over the last century or so would have given only limited insights on this front, because there had been relatively few major financial crises. At any rate, in the secondary banking crisis of the mid-1970s, the amount of 'exceptional' lending was about £3 billion or, at most, 4 per cent of GDP.[20] In the latest crisis, estimating the amount of exceptional lending is more problematic, since the Treasury has invested in banks' preference shares and so assumed part of the Bank of England's traditional lender-of-last-resort role, but a figure under 4 per cent of GDP would be too low.[21] Assuming that any future emergency ought to be not much more than twice as bad as the secondary banking crisis and the latest episode, a reasonable suggestion is that a privatised Bank

---

19   Ray B. Westerfield, *Money, Credit and Banking*, Ronald Press, New York, 1938, p. 386.

20   Reid, op. cit., p. 192.

21   At the time of writing (November 2008) about £10 billion of the Northern Rock loan, the sums implicit in the Bradford & Bingley nationalisation and the government's offer to subscribe to preference capital issues are outstanding. For the author's view on the government's investment in the equity of UK banks, see note 25 to Chapter 5 above.

of England might need – in very extreme circumstances – to be able to acquire assets equal to a maximum of about 10 per cent of GDP. Some of the assets might be risky, including possibly some claims on the private sector with meaningful default risk, but the central bank ought so to conduct its operations that its maximum loss on bad assets in any two- or three-year period is 0.5 to 1 per cent of GDP. In a crisis it ought to be highly profitable in operational terms, i.e. from high net interest receipts, because of the large size of its balance sheet. On this basis central bank capital equal to 1 per cent of GDP ought to be sufficient to deal with any problems in the banking system which might arise in crisis conditions. In the UK today 1 per cent of GDP would be roughly £15 billion.

What about the relationship between the central bank's capital and the capital of the commercial banking system? HSBC includes the old Midland Bank and is headquartered in London, although it is in reality a Hong Kong Chinese bank. If half of HSBC were included in 'the British banking system', the system's total capital would have been about £200 billion before the government-imposed recapitalisation exercise in October 2008. The system's capital in early 2009 may be of the order of £250 billion. If the Bank of England were capitalised on the same lines as the Fed (i.e. 6 per cent of banks' own capital), the implied figure is £15 billion, virtually identical to 1 per cent of GDP. So both approaches – an estimate of maximum balance sheet exposure relative to GDP during an emergency and the adoption of the same basis as the Federal Reserve – point to a desirable capital for a privatised Bank of England of roughly £15 billion.

For much of the time the capital will be unused, in that the Bank's balance sheet will be much less than ten times capital.

Indeed, if all went well, the full capital would never be needed.[22] The American arrangements – in which only half of the due capital has in fact been called – could be copied in this country. To some extent the central bank's capital and the deposit insurance agency's fund serve an overlapping purpose, since both are available to help a commercial bank in trouble. As far as the commercial banks are concerned, an investment in the central bank is surely far more attractive than an obligation to pre-fund a deposit insurance agency. Since the UK coped well for decades until the 1980s without a system of deposit insurance, the intention of the current proposal is that – as far as possible – the task of maintaining financial stability should be concentrated at the Bank of England. The hope would be that effective deployment of its lender-of-last-resort powers would minimise calls on the deposit insurance backstop. It is true that in some circumstances banks' difficulties may be insolvency rather than illiquidity. If so, calls on the deposit insurance fund might become unavoidable. The deposit insurance agency should, however, be housed in the same building as the Bank of England, and in the UK and elsewhere the deposit insurance agency and the central bank should always work together.[23]

22　Each member bank would have a claim on the Bank of England equal to, say, 3 per cent of its capital, plus an obligation to subscribe a further 3 per cent in certain conditions. If the Bank were facing losses because of a systemic crisis, that might justify the calling of the 3 per cent from *every* member bank. Alternatively, in extreme circumstances the central bank might use the threat to call capital from *one* misbehaving but recalcitrant member bank as a means of bringing it to heel.

23　In the USA the Federal Reserve and FDIC have to work closely together in bank rescues, even if the relations between them are sometimes fraught. Further complexity arises from possible interventions by the Office of the Comptroller of the Currency. Irvine Sprague, chairman of the FDIC for over eleven years to 1986, said in a 1986 book that 'the incredible tangle of jurisdictional overlap' justified 'a major restructuring of the agencies – consolidation'. Sprague, *Bailout*, Beard Books, Washington, DC, 1986, p. 231.

Central banking and debt management

A few words need to be added here about the type of assets that the Bank is to buy from the commercial banks when it does make outright purchases. Since the Bank ought to avoid risk as far as possible, the obvious assets for the purpose of open-market operations are government securities. It follows that at all times the commercial banks ought to hold a liquidity cushion in the form of government securities.[24] As was shown early in Chapter 6, this was true throughout the twentieth century, except at its very end. Further, the Bank has to ensure that the government issues a sufficiently large quantity of Treasury bills and short-dated gilts to meet the banking system's needs. By implication, the Bank must be involved in the management of the public debt and, in particular, it has to monitor the debt's maturity profile. As was also shown in Chapter 6, the failure of the British government, and more specifically of the Debt Management Office (DMO), to issue significant quantities of short-dated government securities in the middle years of the current decade goes a long way to explain British banks' disastrous foray into structured finance products. They bought triple-A mortgage-backed paper as a form of liquidity largely because official policy had caused a shortage of their traditional liquid assets.

Given the DMO's mistake, King's requirement in August 2007 that banks use government securities in repos was to add insult to injury. Nevertheless, as ever it has to be said that errors in policymaking reflect background institutions and recent history, and should not be blamed solely on individuals. The decision to withdraw debt management from the Bank of England's remit,

---

24   Eligible bills also have a role, but the discussion would become complicated. See note 6 to Chapter 6 above.

and to place it with a DMO uninterested in monetary policy, was taken in 1997 by a government that had only just been elected. None of the politicians in that government had any meaningful in-depth technical knowledge of debt management or could argue with Treasury officials who resented the extent of the powers (i.e. to set interest rates) being handed over to the newly independent Bank of England. So the responsibility to manage the public debt was taken from the Bank in an arbitrary and misjudged bureaucratic carve-up. Debt management needs to be integrated with the rest of monetary policy again, and the Bank of England must have a major influence over the instrument composition and maturity structure of the national debt. Of course, it has to work with the Treasury, since the debt is the government's and the minimisation of debt-interest costs is a valid objective of public policy. But – since debt-interest costs are a transfer from one group of citizens to another – the minimisation of debt-interest costs is far less important than maintaining the stability of the banking system.[25]

25 According to a section on the Debt Management Office's website, it has eight strategic objectives for 2008/09. Debt management matters to the central bank both because it affects the availability of assets suitable for inclusion in banks' assets (i.e. financial stability) and because it impacts on the rate of growth of the quantity of money (i.e. monetary stability). (When a bank acquires a claim on the government, the government's bank deposit increases in the first instance. But – when the deposit has been spent – that expands the deposits held by the private sector, which are money.) Neither financial nor monetary stability was mentioned in the DMO's eight strategic objectives. The relationship between debt management on the one hand and financial stability and monetary stability on the other is often misunderstood or even denied. (For a perhaps surprising example, see Stanley Fischer, 'Modern central banking', in Forrest Capie et al., *The Future of Central Banking*, Cambridge University Press, Cambridge, 1994, pp. 262–308, especially p. 302 and p. 304.) The case for integrating debt management with monetary policy is made in David B. Smith, *Cracks in the Foundations?*, Economic Research Council, London, 2007.

The central bank and banking regulation

Chapter 3 showed that banks do their utmost to minimise cash holdings, even though they must always have at least some cash among their assets. Subsequent chapters have demonstrated that, if the central bank is to help them in the minimisation of their cash holdings, they need at all times to have a buffer of assets that can be sold outright – quickly, with little fuss and with almost complete certainty about their nominal value – to the central bank for cash. Clearly, the central bank must have information about commercial banks' cash holdings and the likely pattern of cash movements in and out of their central bank balance over the next few weeks, and also about the size and composition of the buffer of liquid assets that are available for sale, perhaps to it.

In an extreme crisis, with a major run on a particular bank's cash holdings, a commercial bank may lose all its original cash and be forced to sell its liquid assets to the central bank for cash, and yet may lose all that cash too: we are talking about an extreme crisis, but this is roughly what happened with Northern Rock. The central bank then has no option. It must either lend, on last-resort terms, to the bank in question or persuade strongly placed commercial banks to take its place via an inter-bank facility. If the deed is not done on its own balance sheet, but via a support line in the inter-bank market, it may have to give a guarantee on that line.[26] Of course, the central bank can be confident of repayment (and/or that its guarantee will not be called) only if it knows that the borrowing bank is solvent. Not only must the bank's assets be

---

26　In the small banks crisis in the early 1990s the Bank of England once guaranteed a bank's liabilities without the bank itself being told! (witness statement of Ian Bond, in the action between Northern Rock claimants and HM Treasury, 31 July 2008, clause 29).

of high quality and with a clear margin of collateral, but also the figure for the bank's equity capital in its latest accounts must be correct. It follows that the central bank must have information about the troubled bank's loan and securities portfolios, the basis on which its accounts were prepared and a host of other details.

More succinctly, the central bank's lender-of-last-resort role presupposes an extensive and continuous exchange of information between it and the commercial banks to which it may, in certain circumstances, have to lend. From the beginning of the Bank of England's assumption of the lender-of-last-resort role in the nineteenth century until 1998 the Bank was responsible for the supervision of commercial bank balance sheets and the regulation of the banking system. The logic of the arrangement was so obviously blessed by experience and is so clear cut in its practical rationale that it is puzzling that any alternative could even have been considered.[27] The transfer of banking supervision and regulation from the Bank of England to a new and untried institution, the Financial Services Authority, in the 1998 Bank of England Act and the 2000 Financial Services and Markets Act was wrongheaded. At that time central banking and the regulation of the commercial banking system had been separated in some countries, such as Germany, but these countries did not generally have an outstanding record in the provision of banking services. The Bank of England's powers as a bank supervisor and regulator need to be restored. If lender-of-last resort loans are to be extended only to solvent banking institutions, the Bank of England needs to know enough about their businesses to be certain that they are in

27 The question was discussed in paras 83–103 of the first volume of the Treasury and Civil Service Committee's report *The Role of the Bank of England*, HMSO, London, 1993.

fact solvent. By extension, the Bank of England needs to employ a sufficient number of people of sufficient seniority, qualifications and experience to discharge its duties as banking regulator.

A possible criticism of the proposal is that, if the regulatory role of a privatised Bank of England were to be reinstated, it would have to be done by statute and a privately owned body would have virtual police powers over the British banking system.[28] But the UK financial sector had a long record of self-regulation under the law until the 1980s. Further, there is nothing new about a private body enforcing by-laws on a group of individuals or companies that have voluntarily agreed to accept its jurisdiction in certain matters. The self-generation of regulation by market institutions has a long tradition, not least in financial markets. Of course, if the central bank is oppressive in bank regulation, the owners of the commercial banks can register their protests in various ways, not least by switching their capital abroad. A privately owned Bank of England would not want to alienate its shareholders and its key stakeholders, namely the UK commercial banking industry.

Checks and balances in a system with a privatised Bank of England

The remainder of this chapter will offer some remarks on how a privatised Bank of England might be organised. It should be reiterated that, despite having private shareholders, the Bank's functions and operations would still to a large extent be specified in a parliamentary statute. On the monetary stability front, that

---

28   In the USA before the founding of the Federal Reserve the clearing-house associations carried out bank examinations to check loan quality. C. Arthur Phillips, *Bank Credit*, Macmillan, New York, 1921, pp. 302–9.

would of course be inescapable. More awkward questions might seem to arise with regard to financial stability. Would a privatised Bank of England have a meaningful incentive to maintain financial stability? If it were owned by the banks, might it not be a soft touch (on such matters as access to central bank credit, rules on capital, and so on) and allow them to take undue liberties in the conduct of their businesses?

The answer is provided partly by historical experience. The Bank of England was privately owned from 1694 to 1946, and it was recognised as a different kind of institution from other banks, as a central bank rather than a commercial bank, from about the 1860s to 1946. These were the years in which it established a reputation as both a staunch defender of monetary stability (mostly by its adhesion to the gold standard), and as the guardian of the safety of bank deposits in Britain and so of financial stability more generally. Conflicts had arisen in the early nineteenth century between its maintenance of the two kinds of stability and its profit-making responsibilities to shareholders, but after Bagehot's work its special position was understood. No insuperable conflicts arose from the late nineteenth century until 1946 between private ownership and the Bank's delivery of financial stability. Similarly, in the USA the Federal Reserve has been able since the mid-1930s to reconcile its ownership status with an acceptable record on financial stability. In recent decades the worst solvency problems among US deposit-taking institutions have occurred not in commercial banking, but in the savings and loans industry (i.e. in specialist housing finance intermediaries), in the state-sponsored mortgage guarantee businesses known colloquially as Fannie Mae and Freddie Mac, and in investment banks such as Lehman Brothers. None of these entities was supervised by the Fed.

Indeed, a case can be made that a central bank owned by the commercial banks ought to have a benign incentive structure. Chapter 3 discussed banks' almost unremitting efforts over the long run to lower their ratios of cash and liquid assets to total assets, and also their ratios of capital to assets, and argued that 'low-ratio banking' (as it might be termed) cut the cost of services, including loan margins, to banks' customers. With the Bank of England owned by the UK's leading banking groups, they would press for the ratios to be as low as possible, while remaining consistent with balance-sheet safety. As explained in Chapter 4, one result ought to be narrow loan margins that benefit companies, homeowners and other borrowers. The banks would also be keen to formalise lender-of-last-resort arrangements with the Bank of England and to put them on a definite contractual basis, so that the misunderstandings of the summer of 2007 do not recur. In summary, the commercial banks would want the Bank of England to act, more explicitly than it now does, as a bank that – from time to time – can expand its balance sheet aggressively and so prevent misplaced worries about solvency poisoning inter-bank relationships.

On the other hand, both the banks and the Bank of England would have a strong interest in the continuation of safe banking. Since the commercial banks would be the Bank's shareholders, they would want its operations to be profitable. If heavy losses were recorded because assets of poor quality were purchased in support operations or because last-resort loans were made to genuinely insolvent banks, prudent and risk-averse banks would have to provide extra capital to cover the Bank of England's short-fall. The banks would have to work together, at least to some extent, like the members of a club. Lazy and incompetent central banking could allow risky and irresponsible commercial banking. The cautious banks would want the Bank of England to monitor and restrain risky behaviour by a rigorous system of peer review. Over the last few years Lloyds TSB is widely thought to have been more solid and risk averse than, say, the Royal Bank of Scotland or HBOS, and its aversion to risk has helped it to weather the crisis better than its rivals. The structure of regulation over the last decade, however, did not penalise irresponsible behaviour until a major crisis was under way. If a more explicit system of club rules had been in place, the crisis might not have happened.

In the sort of world being discussed here the greater the Bank of England's success, the less it would appear in the news. Its balance sheet in normal conditions would have only trivial claims on the banking system. On the liabilities side of the balance sheet it would have capital (equal, as discussed, to about 1 per cent of GDP), the note issue (perhaps 3 per cent of GDP), banks' own balances for clearing purposes (say 0.25 per cent of GDP, if that) and the government's balance (again 0.25 per cent of GDP, if that), while government securities of about 4.5 per cent of GDP and a tiny working balance of notes would constitute all of its assets. Repo items can be ignored, as they cancel out in any meaningful sense. The profits on the note issue and the government's own balance (i.e. the interest earned on the government securities, to the extent of 3.25 per cent of GDP in the illustration) would of course be returned to the government. The distribution of the income on the Bank's own capital, and banks' own cash reserve balances, would be largely a matter for the shareholders (i.e. the commercial banks). But arrangements could to be made, first, to ensure that the top central bankers receive incomes not much different from those of senior executives in the banking industry (perhaps on a long-term bonus arrangement that kicks in as more years free of crisis and with on-target inflation are recorded) and, second, to retain teams of officials that collectively have thousands of years of central banking expertise. In the USA 95 per cent of the Fed's profits are returned to the state, apparently with only limited incentive arrangements for the staff. In the author's view central bank staff should have strong incentives to perform well. The USA's misplaced reliance on a too-extensive deposit insurance system also muddies the waters.

What would happen if there were a big crisis? With capital at 1 per cent of GDP, the aim would be that the Bank of England could add last-resort loans to its assets up to a limit of 10 per cent of GDP. Alternatively, it ought to be able to purchase securities to the same extent and with the same objective (i.e. the maintenance of financial stability) in view. The Bank must be able to do this on its own initiative, without any reference to politicians or civil servants. Since the UK banking system's own capital would not usually be much in excess of 10 per cent of GDP, and good regulation should ensure that banks are solvent anyhow, the likelihood of a systemic crisis blowing the whole system away – and so requiring an appeal to the state – ought to be negligible.[29]

29   What if, without good reason, people became concerned that a solvent banking system was insolvent and started to convert deposits into notes on a very large scale (say, 20 or 30 per cent of GDP)? (The cancellation of inter-bank lines, as in 2007 and 2008, might have much the same effect on the banks, since each individual bank would feel that its cash was being drained.) Then the central bank should extend loans to the banks to replace the lost deposits and the system can wait for the deposits to return. The deposits will return when people realise that the banks are in fact solvent, and miss the interest paid and transactions convenience of having their wealth in the form of bank deposits rather than cash. But – clearly – if the central bank's balance sheet ballooned to 20 or 30 per cent of GDP, the circumstances would be extraordinary, and the central bank would need to review the matter with the government and legislature. As noted in the

It has to be admitted that, in a full-blown crisis in which the prices of assets (such as houses and commercial property) widely used as bank collateral fell by between (say) 30 to 50 per cent in a one-year or two-year period, any central bank would have difficulty maintaining financial stability. If a crisis of this sort occurred, the proposed system – in which the central bank is owned by the banking system, and is responsible for both monetary and financial stability – would have failed. The Bank of England's senior executives, including its governor, deputy governors and so on, would be sacked without any long-term bonuses being paid. Of course, the losses to them, in terms of both reputation and money, would be severe. The threat of that ought to encourage the Bank's management team both to supervise and regulate the banks with great care, and to achieve a satisfactory degree of macroeconomic stability. As with any well-designed constitutional order, a privately owned central bank would be subject to checks and balances, and these checks and balances could be tweaked with experience to improve the outcomes. It is difficult to believe that the proposed system – which recalls the Bank of England's own past success – could lead to a disaster worse than the UK banking debacle of 2007 and 2008.

Central banking in a liberal financial system

The proposed model, a privately owned central bank with extensive responsibilities for both the regulation of the banking system

---

text (pp. 142–3 above], King has denied that the central bank can provide long-term finance to banks. It is precisely in crisis circumstances – when the system is solvent, but a run develops because of 'the fear of fear itself' – that King's doctrine is most dangerous.

and the management of the public debt, may appear to concentrate too much power in one place. But – emphatically – this would be central banking for a free society. Because the Bank of England would be in private ownership but subject to statute, its governor and senior executives would answer simultaneously to shareholders with money at stake and to democratically elected politicians. If the Bank's officers abused their powers, they could quickly be brought to heel. Chapter 5 argued that the era of constructive ambiguity in last-resort lending must end, and advocated instead a clear contractual framework for transactions between the central bank and the rest of the banking system. The result would be a better balance of power between them, which ought to prevent arbitrary and dictatorial behaviour by the governor of the Bank of England in a financial crisis. Whether King was too hostile towards the banks in late 2007 and 2008 can be debated. But, without question, many senior executives in the banking industry resented the treatment they received.

The current UK arrangements are distinctly illiberal. A government agency, the Financial Services Authority, has more or less unlimited regulatory powers. A case can be argued that, in the bank recapitalisation exercise of October 2008, those powers were seriously misapplied. No one knows whether the current downturn in the UK economy will be long lasting, but the UK's banks were mandated to raise large amounts of capital and so to anticipate the loan losses of a severe recession. Given the trauma then prevailing in financial markets, the banks' own shareholders did not have the funds available to subscribe for all the new shares. The government was able to buy large equity stakes in Royal Bank of Scotland, HBOS and Lloyds TSB at prices beneath asset value per share, implying massive dilution of existing shareholders' assets. The government's actions may have been legal, but they challenged private property rights and insulted the rule of law.

The proposed system would be voluntary, in that financial organisations could choose whether or not to have a relationship with the Bank of England. There is nothing inherently coercive in an arrangement whereby commercial banks receive services from the central bank (which helps them run the payments system and provides last-resort lending), and in return submit themselves to a set of club rules. All contracts are a mixture of give and take, and this relationship would have to be subject to contract. As long as the club's rules (on asset composition and solvency, among other matters) are enforced in the same way for all its members, the commercial banks ought to be able to work closely and amicably with the central bank.

The aim would not be to achieve desired outcomes by forcing the central bank and the banking industry to behave in certain ways. On the contrary, the intention of privatising the Bank of England, and returning to it powers that it once exercised with great success, would be to facilitate the wider promotion of a liberal financial system. Within that system the main players would be free to make most key choices according to their own interests, but – as in Adam Smith's system of natural liberty – with socially beneficial results. To repeat, the proposal is, above all, about the organisation of central banking in a free society.

8 CONCLUSION: THE CASE FOR A 'BROAD' CENTRAL BANK

The analysis in this study may disappoint strong believers in the freedom of the individual and limited government interference in the economy. One of its conclusions is to reject Hayek's call for the denationalisation of money and the repeal of the legal-tender laws. Instead the study endorses the issue of legal-tender notes by a unique kind of institution, a central bank, which relies on statutory backing. Other arguments here may upset those critics of central banking who, from a free-market perspective, would like all banks to be on the same footing. This study asserts that, on the contrary, economic efficiency is served by a clear differentiation between commercial banks that maximise profits and the central bank charged with public policy objectives. It accepts – in line with the prevailing political consensus – that these objectives are twofold, monetary stability (to keep the value of its liabilities stable in real terms) and financial stability (to maintain the convertibility of bank deposits into its own note liabilities). Further, it acknowledges that the central bank must be accountable to the legislature, and must even from time to time cooperate with the executive (specifically the finance ministry) over such matters of mutual concern as the management of the public debt. So, this very special and unusual institution awkwardly straddles the public and private sectors. Its operations lie in the sphere of profit-making business and finance, while its status and performance are part of the political debate. It can have none of the purity, simplicity and supposed automaticity of central banking, as this activity is sometimes envisaged by free-market economists.[1]

Why 100 per cent systems don't work

Moreover, the present study has questioned the attractions of 100 per cent reserve banking and its contemporary version of 'narrow banking', both of which may be seen as expressions of Currency School thinking. To recall the quotation from Phillips' classic on *Bank Credit*, the essence of banking is to expand earning assets as much as possible relative to both cash and capital.[2] Banks are driven in this direction by their attempts to maximise the rate of return on capital. The lessons of history are clear cut, that profit maximisation is all powerful and 100-per-cent-backed systems in their various forms always break down. Sooner or later free markets develop a money substitute for the 100-per-cent-backed 'money' asset, the quantities of this substitute become enormous relative to the 100-per-cent-backed money, and sudden large-scale conversions of the money substitute into the 100-per-cent-backed money overwhelm the system, usually in crisis conditions. One hundred per cent systems are sometimes advertised as foolproof and unsinkable. In practice, they hit an iceberg in the form of mass exchanges of the money substitute back into the supposedly 100 per cent safe 'money'

---

1   For a recent critique of central banking, from the standpoint of an advocate of 100-per-cent-reserve-backed money, see Jesus Huerta de Soto, *Money, Bank Credit, and Economic Cycles*, Ludwig von Mises Institute, Auburn, AL, 2006 (originally published in Spanish in 1998).

2   See p. 42 above.

asset. The imposition of a 100 per cent reserve requirement on all notes, on all sight deposits or on all deposits nowhere guarantees monetary and financial stability.

If a 100 per cent bullion reserve requirement is imposed on notes (as under England's 1844 Bank Charter Act), the central bank and its customers remain free to expand the central bank's deposit liabilities, and the convertibility of these deposit liabilities into notes may lead to a run on the notes which exhausts the gold, as it did more or less in 1847, 1857 and 1866. If a 100 per cent reserve requirement is set on sight deposits (as recommended by Irving Fisher and the 'narrow bankers'), the commercial banks and their customers remain free to expand their time deposits, and the convertibility of the time deposits into sight deposits and so ultimately into cash may lead to a total withdrawal of banks' cash holdings. If a nation establishes a currency board and orders its central bank to match its note liabilities entirely by dollars, the nation's commercial banks remain free to expand their deposit liabilities without any dollar backing, and the convertibility of deposits into notes and so into dollars may result in the total depletion of the central bank's dollar assets, as happened to Chile's currency board in 1982 and Argentina's in 2002.[3]

Attempts to ensure financial stability by 100 per cent systems are often attempts to prohibit 'banking', in that credit creation is meant to occur outside institutions that call themselves 'banks'. They may work for a time, but in the long run they disintegrate. Surprising though it may seem, banking has one characteristic

---

3   For Chile's woes, in which the privatisation of the banking system had to be reversed by wholesale renationalisation after a wild boom-bust cycle, see Tim Congdon, *Economic Liberalism in the Cone of Latin America*, Trade Policy Research Centre, London, 1985, pp. 90–98.

in common with alcohol consumption, drug taking and prosti-
tution. No matter the strictness with which officialdom tries to
restrict and control it, banking – the operation of a deposit-taking
and lending system with a reserve of well under 100 per cent – is
irrepressible. It always resurfaces in another place or reappears in
much the same form, if with a different label. Chapters 4 and 5 of
this study documented bankers' persistent and successful efforts,
over periods of decades and even centuries, to lower their cash
and capital ratios. The two chapters also explained why low-ratio
banking was good for economic welfare, in that it lowered the cost
of banking services to non-banks. Further, the analysis there identified the origin of banks' demand for a central banking function.
It is because banks want to economise on their cash and capital,
and yet still of course be able to repay deposits over the counter,
that they have a demand for central bank services.

The historical record cannot be gainsaid.[4] A nation with a
privately owned, profit-oriented banking system but without a
central bank will evolve, as a matter of free choice, in the direction of central banking. People in one nation do not like having to
buy and sell in a multiplicity of monies, but favour one monetary
standard, a single currency taking the form of a legal-tender note
issue emanating from a state-sponsored bank. As far as possible
they make this money work for them, either reducing their transactions costs or paying a rate of interest, by leaving a fraction of it
deposited with a commercial bank. The benefits of the uniqueness

---

4   The development of central banking has varied between countries, being con-
     ditioned by the interaction with other institutions. But the persistence of the
     process, and the tendency to arrive at a similar eventual outcome, is difficult to
     escape. See Forrest Capie et al., *The Future of Central Banking*, Cambridge Uni-
     versity Press, Cambridge, pp. 123–231, 1994, for potted histories of central bank
     development in over thirty countries.

of a 'money' are similar to those of the uniqueness of a system of weights and measures, as Hayek noted in his *Constitution of Liberty*.[5] Once banks exist, a seemingly remorseless pattern of specialisation then develops, in which a variety of interest groups want the bank of issue to be split off from the commercial banks and to be transformed into a central bank.

The central bank as a dominant protective association

Are the resulting arrangements a spontaneous or an imposed order? The order is spontaneous, at least in one sense. In those countries – particularly the UK – which led in the development of central banking, no one had foreseen the eventual outcome when the Bank of England was set up in 1694. Admittedly, the order can be regarded as imposed in a different sense, since its growth and change have been conditioned by legislation, and hence by politics and lobbying. The issue depends on how words are used and so is at least partly semantic. But surely the free banking school must accept that the rule of law, and so the passage of legislation, is an inevitable feature of all societies, no matter how uncompromising their commitment to personal liberty. Central banking is no more inconsistent with a free society than the rule of law. Further, the process by which the central bank becomes the dominant and eventually the sole issuer of legal-tender banknotes is related to the process by which commercial banks select the central bank, the bank of issue, as their banker, the bankers' bank. In due course this bank assumes a responsibility to act as their

---

5   Friedrich Hayek, *The Constitution of Liberty*, University of Chicago Press, Chicago, 1960, pp. 324–9.

lender of last resort.[6] Arguably, these patterns resemble those which, according to Nozick in his classic libertarian statement *Anarchy, State and Utopia*, result in a single 'dominant protective agency' emerging from a chaos of semi-permanent civil warfare and strife, and establishing peace under the law.[7] A central bank is an integral part of a modern market economy, just as law courts are needed to enforce the law and protect property rights.

Alternative central banking structures

But the case for the existence of a central bank does not close down discussion about its possible structure, constitutional position and ownership. Two extremes – two ideal types – might be distinguished, a 'narrow central bank' and a 'broad central bank'. Before developing the distinction, however, it must be understood that the free banking school is right on one point. A modern economy could function without a central bank. It would function badly, with a less efficient banking system and a more expensive payments mechanism, but life would go on.

6   The author first made this argument in a paper published in 1981 (Tim Congdon, 'Is the provision of a sound currency a necessary function of the state?', *National Westminster Quarterly Review*, August 1981). One of the fundamental questions raised by the UK banking crisis of 2007 and 2008 is whether the lender-of-last-resort function will increasingly be shared between the Bank of England and the UK government, because the Bank does not have the capital resources to carry out a last-resort role autonomously. More pithily, what will banks do if the central bank refuses to act as lender of last resort?

7   The emergence of a 'dominant protective association' by a so-called 'invisible hand explanation' was described in Chapter 2 of Robert Nozick, *Anarchy, State and Utopia*, Basil Blackwell, Oxford, 1974. The invocation of Nozick's argument in the author's 1981 article (note 6 above) was intended as a deliberate challenge to the free banking argument, with central banking emerging as the result of 'the invisible hand' that Hayekians so much admire.

Chapter 3 examined the workings of the US economy before 1914, with a large number of private note-issuing banks collaborating in settlement via clearing houses. In the USA of that era numerous note issues – issues by banks, issues by states, issues from the federal government and, as we have seen, even issues by the clearing-house associations – overlapped and competed.[8] But there is a very different possibility. This is for a single legal-tender note issue to be put into circulation by the finance ministry, not the central bank. Although no specific bank of issue exists, deposit-taking, fractional-reserve banking and clearing could all take place. Privately owned banks could meet and reach an agreement that one, two, three or more of their number are particularly strong institutions (which might be called 'money centre banks' or whatever) and that all of them would maintain clearing balances. As the finance ministry would monopolise the note issue, it could set the position of the supply curve of this monetary base asset, just as the central bank does at present. It could therefore control interest rates, even if the context of the transactions differed radically from present-day open-market operations under the central bank's aegis.

This may all seem fanciful, but in World War I the Bank of England and the Treasury quarrelled about their respective roles. The Treasury started to issue notes in its own name (which became known as 'Bradburys', after one of the permanent secretaries of the day who signed the notes) and used them to cover the government's heavy military expenditure. The Bank had to

---

8   Without a central bank after the dissolution of the Second Bank of the United States in 1833, the US Treasury performed semi-central banking functions. See Richard Timberlake, *Monetary Policy in the United States*, University of Chicago Press, Chicago and London, 1978, pp. 74–82.

tolerate the coexistence of its own and the Treasury's notes, even though by 1918 the Treasury's note issue was much larger than its own and a rampant inflation had developed. After much tension and disagreement, which was aggravated by the mistaken decision to return to the gold standard in 1925, the note issue was again consolidated in the Bank of England's name in 1928.[9] But it would have been feasible – perfectly feasible – for the Bank of England to have been wound up in the 1920s and for the Treasury itself to have become the monopoly issuer of banknotes. Business could continue, even in today's world of sophisticated financial markets, without a central bank at all.

With that point established, the distinction between narrow and broad central banking can be drawn. A 'narrow central bank' is to be understood as one that is little more than an interest-rate-setting, note-issuing branch of the executive; it is in reality a department of the Treasury, even if it pretends to be more than that by name. This kind of central bank – in line with Ricardo's *Plan for a National Bank* – would be the only bank entitled to issue legal-tender notes. Deposit-taking commercial banks might find it convenient to deposit notes with it to facilitate clearing, and in this respect it would be a banker's bank. Again in line with Ricardo's vision, however, the central bank's assets would consist exclusively of government securities. Since the central bank could not lend to the private sector, it could not be a lender of last resort. Of course, repo operations in government securities could take place on first-resort terms and these would be sufficient to set interest rates. Advice on the appropriate level of interest rates could be given by an economic research department, while the

---

9   Richard Sayers, *The Bank of England 1891–1944*, Cambridge University Press, Cambridge, 1976, vol. 1, pp. 284–96.

actual decision on interest rates could be reached in a committee of the great and the good, which perhaps (as at present) would be called the Monetary Policy Committee. The central bank would have nothing much to do with banking supervision and regulation, it would have no input into decisions on the maturity profile and instrument composition of the public debt, and it would delegate the complex management matters arising when banks get into trouble to quite separate specialist agencies (i.e. the agencies responsible for the resolution of failed banks and deposit insurance).

A justified interpretation, on the basis of his speeches and public statements, is that Mervyn King would like the Bank of England to be run as a narrow central bank along Ricardian lines. The central bank's output would consist of little more than a particularly important and influential body of economic research. According to Brummer in *The Crunch*, relying on the testimony of 'insiders', King was 'cock-a-hoop' in 1997 when the government decided to take away the Bank's responsibilities for banking regulation and debt management.[10] As a narrow central bank organisation would not interact in any meaningful way with the privately owned banking system and have no meaningful commercial risks on its balance sheet, its ownership makes little difference to its behaviour. For simplicity and continuity, it might as well remain in the state's hands.

The thesis of this study is that a very different type of central bank – a 'broad central bank' – is likely to make a far more positive contribution to economic efficiency. Ricardo and his many Currency School successors saw the debates from a

10   Alex Brummer, *The Crunch*, Random House Business Books, London, 2008, p. 103.

policymaker's perspective. They failed to recognise, first, that a financial system includes thousands of private agents who favour structures that maximise their profits and, second, that these agents' profit-seeking efforts take society closer to a welfare-maximising optimum. The banking industry will invariably favour a bank of issue that has the power, in certain circumstances, to make large loans to solvent banks facing a run; it will always prefer the active vision of central banking expressed in Bagehot's *Lombard Street* to the passivity envisaged in Ricardo's *Plan for a National Bank*. Bankers may believe that, when central banks are able to act as lenders of last resort, that makes possible low-ratio banking, which is good for their profits. As Chapter 4 showed, the true beneficiaries of the lender-of-last-resort role and low-ratio banking are the millions of people and companies who are the banks' customers.

But, while the social cost–benefit arithmetic of central banking is most favourable when it is able to act as a Bagehotian lender of last resort, lender-of-last-resort lending does carry some risks. In return for the collective good of lender-of-last-resort facilities, the central bank is entitled to impose conditions on the businesses that wish to take advantage of those facilities. Fair analogies are with a golf club that has membership rules, and derivatives exchanges and clearing houses that have rule books and by-laws. The central bank must be able to supervise commercial banks, and to some extent to regulate their funding strategies and asset selection. In particular, it is essential that at all times commercial banks have not only a first line of defence against a run in the form of cash, but also a second line of defence in the form of a buffer of liquid assets. Realistically, such assets are most likely to be liquid if they are government securities. The central bank must therefore be closely involved in public debt management, in order that a sufficient quantity of Treasury bills and short-dated government securities are issued for the banks' purposes. All being well, good management decisions within the commercial banking industry – in association with effective banking supervision and regulation by the central bank, the appropriate supply of liquid securities to the banks by the managers of the public debt and the occasional last-resort facility to ease liquidity strains – ought to prevent any bank 'going bust'. If so, the deposit insurance agency and a special bank resolution regime will be unemployed and irrelevant.[11]

If that seems like a pipe dream in early 2009, it must be emphasised that between 1866 and the early 1990s not one significant British bank went bust in a way that embarrassed the state. At no point in these many decades did UK bank customers require protection, on a large scale, from a specially created deposit insurance fund.[12] The pressures on central bank executives to deliver financial stability are likely to be most powerful if the central bank is privately owned. Specifically, the Bank of England, like the USA's Federal Reserve, should be owned by the banks and be financially accountable to them. The banking industry has a strong interest in the encouragement of a group of long-term career central banking professionals. People who decide to make a career out of central banking must be both familiar with the problems of privately owned commercial banks, and answerable by statute to the legislature to achieve monetary and financial stability.

---

11 The redundancy of the deposit insurance agency and the special resolution regime would be due, ultimately, to macroeconomic stability and the successful allocation of resources by the banking system.

12 In the early 1990s UK citizens did lose money on deposits held at the Bank of Credit and Commerce International, often at UK-based branches, but BCCI was in fact regulated (if that is the right word) in Luxembourg, not the UK.

The case for the Bank of England to become a broad central bank in private ownership may seem radical and daring, even something of a leap in the dark. But – compared with some of the ideas of the free banking school – the proposal is highly conservative. All that is being advocated is the restoration of the kind of central banking arrangements that existed in the UK until 1946 and which do now exist, although perhaps not to the full ideal extent, in the USA. Bluntly, the division of responsibilities and functions between the Tripartite Authorities, due to misguided legislation in 1998 and 2000, has led to the UK's worst financial catastrophe since the South Sea Bubble. The privatisation of the Bank of England, and its recovery of powers that it exercised successfully for decades, would not be a leap in the dark. Instead it would be the reinstatement of arrangements which were a great practical success and were widely admired across the world.

ABOUT THE IEA

The Institute is a research and educational charity (No. CC 235 351), limited by guarantee. Its mission is to improve understanding of the fundamental institutions of a free society by analysing and expounding the role of markets in solving economic and social problems.

The IEA achieves its mission by:

- a high-quality publishing programme
- conferences, seminars, lectures and other events
- outreach to school and college students
- brokering media introductions and appearances

The IEA, which was established in 1955 by the late Sir Antony Fisher, is an educational charity, not a political organisation. It is independent of any political party or group and does not carry on activities intended to affect support for any political party or candidate in any election or referendum, or at any other time. It is financed by sales of publications, conference fees and voluntary donations.

In addition to its main series of publications the IEA also publishes a quarterly journal, *Economic Affairs*.

The IEA is aided in its work by a distinguished international Academic Advisory Council and an eminent panel of Honorary Fellows. Together with other academics, they review prospective IEA publications, their comments being passed on anonymously to authors. All IEA papers are therefore subject to the same rigorous independent refereeing process as used by leading academic journals.

IEA publications enjoy widespread classroom use and course adoptions in schools and universities. They are also sold throughout the world and often translated/reprinted.

Since 1974 the IEA has helped to create a worldwide network of 100 similar institutions in over 70 countries. They are all independent but share the IEA's mission.

Views expressed in the IEA's publications are those of the authors, not those of the Institute (which has no corporate view), its Managing Trustees, Academic Advisory Council members or senior staff.

Members of the Institute's Academic Advisory Council, Honorary Fellows, Trustees and Staff are listed on the following page.

The Institute gratefully acknowledges financial support for its publications programme and other work from a generous benefaction by the late Alec and Beryl Warren.

Other papers recently published by the IEA include:

A Market in Airport Slots
Keith Boyfield (editor), David Starkie, Tom Bass & Barry Humphreys
Readings 56; ISBN 0 255 36505 5; £10.00

Money, Inflation and the Constitutional Position of the Central Bank
Milton Friedman & Charles A. E. Goodhart
Readings 57; ISBN 0 255 36538 1; £10.00

railway.com
Parallels between the Early British Railways and the ICT Revolution
Robert C. B. Miller
Research Monograph 57; ISBN 0 255 36534 9; £12.50

The Regulation of Financial Markets
Edited by Philip Booth & David Currie
Readings 58; ISBN 0 255 36551 9; £12.50

Climate Alarmism Reconsidered
Robert L. Bradley Jr
Hobart Paper 146; ISBN 0 255 36541 1; £12.50

Government Failure: E. G. West on Education
Edited by James Tooley & James Stanfield
Occasional Paper 130; ISBN 0 255 36552 7; £12.50

Corporate Governance: Accountability in the Marketplace
Elaine Sternberg
Second edition
Hobart Paper 147; ISBN 0 255 36542 x; £12.50

The Land Use Planning System
Evaluating Options for Reform
John Corkindale
Hobart Paper 148; ISBN 0 255 36550 0; £10.00

Economy and Virtue
Essays on the Theme of Markets and Morality
Edited by Dennis O'Keeffe
Readings 59; ISBN 0 255 36504 7; £12.50

Free Markets Under Siege
Cartels, Politics and Social Welfare
Richard A. Epstein
Occasional Paper 132; ISBN 0 255 36553 5; £10.00

Unshackling Accountants
D. R. Myddelton
Hobart Paper 149; ISBN 0 255 36559 4; £12.50

The Euro as Politics
Pedro Schwartz
Research Monograph 58; ISBN 0 255 36535 7; £12.50

Pricing Our Roads
Vision and Reality
Stephen Glaister & Daniel J. Graham
Research Monograph 59; ISBN 0 255 36562 4; £10.00

The Role of Business in the Modern World
Progress, Pressures, and Prospects for the Market Economy
David Henderson
Hobart Paper 150; ISBN 0 255 36548 9; £12.50

Public Service Broadcasting Without the BBC?
Alan Peacock
Occasional Paper 133; ISBN 0 255 36565 9; £10.00

The ECB and the Euro: the First Five Years
Otmar Issing
Occasional Paper 134; ISBN 0 255 36555 1; £10.00

Towards a Liberal Utopia?
Edited by Philip Booth
Hobart Paperback 32; ISBN 0 255 36563 2; £15.00

The Way Out of the Pensions Quagmire
Philip Booth & Deborah Cooper
Research Monograph 60; ISBN 0 255 36517 9; £12.50

Black Wednesday
A Re-examination of Britain's Experience in the Exchange Rate Mechanism
Alan Budd
Occasional Paper 135; ISBN 0 255 36566 7; £7.50

Crime: Economic Incentives and Social Networks
Paul Ormerod
Hobart Paper 151; ISBN 0 255 36554 3; £10.00

The Road to Serfdom *with* **The Intellectuals and Socialism**
Friedrich A. Hayek
Occasional Paper 136; ISBN 0 255 36576 4; £10.00

Money and Asset Prices in Boom and Bust
Tim Congdon
Hobart Paper 152; ISBN 0 255 36570 5; £10.00

The Dangers of Bus Re-regulation
and Other Perspectives on Markets in Transport
John Hibbs et al.
Occasional Paper 137; ISBN 0 255 36572 1; £10.00

The New Rural Economy
Change, Dynamism and Government Policy
Berkeley Hill et al.
Occasional Paper 138; ISBN 0 255 36546 2; £15.00

The Benefits of Tax Competition
Richard Teather
Hobart Paper 153; ISBN 0 255 36569 1; £12.50

Wheels of Fortune
Self-funding Infrastructure and the Free Market Case for a Land Tax
Fred Harrison
Hobart Paper 154; ISBN 0 255 36589 6; £12.50

Were 364 Economists All Wrong?
Edited by Philip Booth
Readings 60; ISBN 978 0 255 36588 8; £10.00

Europe After the 'No' Votes
Mapping a New Economic Path
Patrick A. Messerlin
Occasional Paper 139; ISBN 978 0 255 36580 2; £10.00

The Railways, the Market and the Government
John Hibbs et al.
Readings 61; ISBN 978 0 255 36567 3; £12.50

Corruption: The World's Big C
Cases, Causes, Consequences, Cures
Ian Senior
Research Monograph 61; ISBN 978 0 255 36571 0; £12.50

Choice and the End of Social Housing
Peter King
Hobart Paper 155; ISBN 978 0 255 36568 0; £10.00

Sir Humphrey's Legacy
Facing Up to the Cost of Public Sector Pensions
Neil Record
Hobart Paper 156; ISBN 978 0 255 36578 9; £10.00

The Economics of Law
Cento Veljanovski
Second edition
Hobart Paper 157; ISBN 978 0 255 36561 1; £12.50

Living with Leviathan
Public Spending, Taxes and Economic Performance
David B. Smith
Hobart Paper 158; ISBN 978 0 255 36579 6; £12.50

The Vote Motive
Gordon Tullock
New edition
Hobart Paperback 33; ISBN 978 0 255 36577 2; £10.00

Waging the War of Ideas
John Blundell
Third edition
Occasional Paper 131; ISBN 978 0 255 36606 9; £12.50

The War Between the State and the Family
How Government Divides and Impoverishes
Patricia Morgan
Hobart Paper 159; ISBN 978 0 255 36596 3; £10.00

Capitalism – A Condensed Version
Arthur Seldon
Occasional Paper 140; ISBN 978 0 255 36598 7; £7.50

Catholic Social Teaching and the Market Economy
Edited by Philip Booth
Hobart Paperback 34; ISBN 978 0 255 36581 9; £15.00

Adam Smith – A Primer
Eamonn Butler
Occasional Paper 141; ISBN 978 0 255 36608 3; £7.50

Happiness, Economics and Public Policy
Helen Johns & Paul Ormerod
Research Monograph 62; ISBN 978 0 255 36600 7; £10.00

They Meant Well
Government Project Disasters
D. R. Myddelton
Hobart Paper 160; ISBN 978 0 255 36601 4; £12.50

Rescuing Social Capital from Social Democracy
John Meadowcroft & Mark Pennington
Hobart Paper 161; ISBN 978 0 255 36592 5; £10.00

Paths to Property
Approaches to Institutional Change in International Development
Karol Boudreaux & Paul Dragos Aligica
Hobart Paper 162; ISBN 978 0 255 36582 6; £10.00

Prohibitions
Edited by John Meadowcroft
Hobart Paperback 35; ISBN 978 0 255 36585 7; £15.00

Trade Policy, New Century
The WTO, FTAs and Asia Rising
Razeen Sally
Hobart Paper 163; ISBN 978 0 255 36544 4; £12.50

Sixty Years On – Who Cares for the NHS?
Helen Evans
Research Monograph 63; ISBN 978 0 255 36611 3; £10.00

Taming Leviathan
Waging the War of Ideas Around the World
Edited by Colleen Dyble
Occasional Paper 142; ISBN 978 0 255 36607 6; £12.50

The Legal Foundations of Free Markets
Edited by Stephen F. Copp
Hobart Paperback 36; ISBN 978 0 255 36591 8; £15.00

Climate Change Policy: Challenging the Activists
Edited by Colin Robinson
Readings 62; ISBN 978 0 255 36595 6; £10.00

Should We Mind the Gap?
Gender Pay Differentials and Public Policy
J. R. Shackleton
Hobart Paper 164; ISBN 978 0 255 36604 5; £10.00

Pension Provision: Government Failure Around the World
Edited by Philip Booth et al.
Readings 63; ISBN 978 0 255 36602 1; £15.00

New Europe's Old Regions
Piotr Zientara
Hobart Paper 165; ISBN 978 0 255 36617 5; £12.50

Other IEA publications

Comprehensive information on other publications and the wider work of the IEA can be found at www.iea.org.uk. To order any publication please see below.

Personal customers

Orders from personal customers should be directed to the IEA:
Bob Layson
IEA
2 Lord North Street
FREEPOST LON10168
London SW1P 3YZ
Tel: 020 7799 8909. Fax: 020 7799 2137
Email: blayson@iea.org.uk

Trade customers

All orders from the book trade should be directed to the IEA's distributor:
Gazelle Book Services Ltd (IEA Orders)
FREEPOST RLYS-EAHU-YSCZ
White Cross Mills
Hightown
Lancaster LA1 4XS
Tel: 01524 68765, Fax: 01524 53232
Email: sales@gazellebooks.co.uk

IEA subscriptions

The IEA also offers a subscription service to its publications. For a single annual payment (currently £42.00 in the UK), subscribers receive every monograph the IEA publishes. For more information please contact:
Adam Myers
Subscriptions
IEA
2 Lord North Street
FREEPOST LON10168
London SW1P 3YZ
Tel: 020 7799 8920, Fax: 020 7799 2137
Email: amyers@iea.org.uk